Twayne's United States Authors Series

Sylvia E. Bowman, *Editor*

INDIANA UNIVERSITY

Captain John Smith

Captain John Smith

CAPTAIN JOHN SMITH

By EVERETT H. EMERSON

University of Massachusetts

TWAYNE PUBLISHERS

A DIVISION OF G. K. HALL & CO., BOSTON, MASS.

973.
210924
Eme

Preface

T O READ Captain John Smith's writings is to enter an exciting period of history and to encounter a complex, striking personality. Smith was a tough-minded dreamer, a practical idealist. He had limitations both as a person and as a writer, but in some ways he is more attractive because of them. He was not a profound thinker, though he was usually serious. (His sense of humor showed itself mostly in irony.) He was a self-made man whose successes were matched by his defeats (not failures); both resulted from luck—good and bad—and his highly developed but limited talents.

Smith's life was that of a story-book hero, an Elizabethan adventurer who found that he could demonstrate his abilities better thousands of miles east or west of England than at home. And he is both charming and infuriating because he slightly but regularly overrated these abilities. Smith wrote mostly because he had had adventures and because he was not able to have any more. His works reflect his pride and his frustration. He did not write much, less than is generally recognized; but considering his education, his profession—that of a soldier—and his life, it is surprising that he wrote as much as he did. Smith has been the subject of nearly thirty biographies, a fact that suggests that his life has fascinated many. Most of these accounts are merely paraphrases of Smith's own autobiographical writings, mixed with a little history; only two biographies, Bradford Smith's and Philip Barbour's, have much scholarship behind them. Uninformed accounts, such as Paul Lewis' *The Great Rogue* (1966), continue to appear.

As a writer Smith has fared even less well. The only fairly detailed books dealing with his writings are Moses Coit Tyler's, which dates from 1878, Howard Mumford Jones' of 1946 (somewhat revised, 1968), and those of Bradford Smith and Barbour. The approaches of the latter two are biographical; the earlier two are out of date and partial. It is time, therefore, that someone undertook an extended study of Smith's works. Perhaps because of this lack, most accounts in literary histories emphasize the man;

remarks about his writings are usually impressionistic and some are misinformed. It is too easy to caricature Smith as an egotistical braggart and liar. Yet the frequent reprinting of Smith's works, in whole or in part, suggests a continuing interest, and of course samples of them are to be found in most anthologies of American literature.

In the following study I have undertaken to consider Smith as a writer. The study does not rest on original biographical research, for the work behind Philip Barbour's excellent life is so thorough that it is unlikely that much of importance remains to be unearthed. I have tried to take advantage of Bradford Smith's and Barbour's work and have had the advantage of helpful conversations and correspondence with Mr. Barbour, who saved me from errors and provided several helpful leads. My approach is, however, different from Barbour's, and what I have to say about John Smith is, of course, my responsibility.

Though Smith wrote only one work in America, one not intended for publication, he is by common consent the first American writer. He was an American, it should be insisted, because his vision of America was what might be considered the characteristic one. He was excited by the possibilities of life in the New World, where a man's status might depend on his own endeavors. This bootstraps philosophy of Smith's is more attractive than most nineteenth-century varieties because it included a perception of the beauties of America and because Smith was without question devoted to high principles. He was also an American in another sense: though he spent less than three of his more than fifty years in America, he has been adopted by later Americans as one of us. Stephen Vincent Benét said it clearly:

> And John Smith went exploring,
> He is one of the first Americans we know,
> And we can claim him, though not by the bond of birth,
> For we've always bred chimeras.
> And he was one,
> This bushy bearded, high-foreheaded, trusting man,
> Who could turn his hand to anything at a pinch,
> Bragging, canny, impatient, durable,
> And fallen in love with the country at first sight.
> For that is something which happens or does not.
> It did to him.[1]

Bradford Smith's explanation of his status as an American is that he is the ideal American hero: "He brings medieval chivalry to the frontier and naturalizes it with us. He stands with one mailed fist extended towards the European past, but with one moccasined foot planted in the American forest. Half knight and half resourceful woodsman, he points the way to the pioneer, the frontiersman ..."[2]

It is difficult not to have strong feelings about Captain John Smith. I confess that I admire him very much, though I frequently find him exasperating. He wrote well, though nearly everything is flawed. He very much needed an editor, a Maxwell Perkins, to set him straight. (He had one once, and the product is Smith's most consistently good piece, "The Description of Virginia.") I have sought to do for Smith three things. First, in Chapter 1 I have tried to establish the context necessary for an understanding of Smith's works. Smith lived a very long time ago, and his life and works were interwoven with the events of his time. The literary background of Smith's historical writings, reports, and propaganda is not well known, even to students of the English literature of Smith's era. Many of these works are fascinating, and some knowledge of them is necessary since Smith himself knew most and used many in preparing his own works. Second, in Chapter 2 I have sought to provide the information about Smith's life and career needed to understand his writings with their strongly autobiographical aspect. Third, I have examined and analyzed the works themselves. In this examination, I have not much emphasized literary criticism; for it is easier to pass judgment on Smith's writings than to understand them. Smith's literary weaknesses are only too apparent: obscurity resulting from omission of necessary words, lack of sense of form, bad grammar, an inability to present reports objectively. Less obvious is, for example, the matter of Smith's originality. How much of the *True Travels* and the *Generall Historie* did Smith write? Wherein is Smith's importance as a writer? What forces shaped the *Historie?* These and similar literary questions I have tried to answer.

Although a modern edition of Smith's writings is much needed, the edition prepared by Edward Arber and A. G. Bradley will suffice: *Travels and Works of Captain John Smith* (Edinburgh, 1910; reprinted New York, 1966). All of my references are to this edition, except for a few to Smith's *Sea Grammar,* which is not included in it. For the *Grammar,* I use the edition included in *The Generall Historie of Virginia, New England & The Summer Isles* (Glasgow, 1907). I have modernized spelling, capitalization, the use of italics, punctuation, and paragraphing.

The portrait of Captain John Smith is from the first state of the map included in *A Description of New England* (1616). The original, in the Clements Library of the University of Michigan, is reproduced here by permission. The lines from *Western Star* by Stephen Vincent Benét are reprinted by permission of Brandt and Brandt. The book is published by Holt, Rinehart, and Winston and copyrighted in 1943 by Rosemary Carr Benét. The texts of Smith's two commendatory poems are based on copies in The Huntington Library, San Marino, California, and used with its permission. Somewhat different versions of my chapters 5 and 7 have been published previously, the former in the *Virginia Magazine of History and Biography;* the latter in the *Early American Literature Newsletter.* I am grateful to the editors for permission to use them in their new form.

For help of various sorts I am indebted to the staffs of the libraries of Harvard University, Brown University, Smith College, Amherst College, Yale University, and the University of Massachusetts, and the Boston Public Library, the Library of Congress, and the Folger Shakespeare Library. I am grateful to the University of Massachusetts for a grant that helped me prepare this study, and to Miss Mary Treacy, an intelligent typist. For many suggestions, I thank Mr. Philip L. Barbour of Newtown, Connecticut; my colleague Professor Morris Golden; Professor William A. Koelsch of Clark University; my wife Katherine and my son Stephen.

EVERETT H. EMERSON

University of Massachusetts

Contents

Preface

Chronology

1. The America of the Elizabethans   13

2. The Place of Writing in Smith's Career   32

3. The Reporter   45

4. The Compiler: The *Generall Historie*   63

5. The Historian: The *Generall Historie*   78

6. The Hack Writer   88

7. The Autobiographer   94

8. The New England Writings   103

9. An Assessment   119

    Notes and References   126

    Selected Bibliography   134

    Index   141

Chronology

1580	Birth of John Smith, eldest son of George Smith, freeman farmer, at Willoughby, in Alford, Lincolnshire, England.
1592–1595	Attended school at nearby Louth.
1595	Apprenticed to a merchant at King's Lynn, Norfolk.
1596	Death of George Smith, with son John inheriting his farm.
1597–1599	Served with English troops in the Netherlands.
1599	As a servant, accompanied Peregrine Bertie, son of the lord of the manor of Willoughby, to France.
1600	Visited Scotland briefly. Returned to Willoughby, where he read Machiavelli's *Art of War* and Antonio de Guevara's *Dial of Princes* and practiced horsemanship. Traveled to the Netherlands, where, after a temporary peace had been reached, he decided to fight in Hungary against the Turks.
1601	Crossed France, took a ship for Italy, and after misadventures, a visit to Alexandria and Greece, and a sea battle which brought him money, reached the French Riviera. Toured Italy (Livorno, Siena, Rome, Naples, Florence, and Venice). Finally reached Vienna and joined the Imperial Army. Assisted in successful battle against the Turks in the Balkans. Made captain of 250 horsetroops.
1602	Continued service against the Turks. Killed three Turks in duels and was given a pension, the right to decorate his shield with three Turks' heads, and the title of English gentleman. Wounded in a later battle, captured, sold as a slave.
1603	Arrived in Constantinople to serve as slave for a girl (Smith's Charatza Trabigzanda). Then shipped across the Black Sea and up the Don River to her brother, who mistreated him. Killed the brother; escaped northward to Muscovy, then to Poland, and finally

back to the Holy Roman Empire, where he was presented money and a document citing his achievements.

1604   Toured Germany, France, Spain, and Morocco, and took part in a sea fight off the African coast.

1605–1606   Returned to England. Worked with Bartholomew Gosnold in making plans for the Virginia colony.

1606   Departed in December for America with over one hundred colonists on three ships.

1607   Arrived in March in the West Indies; in late April, at Chesapeake Bay. Appointed to governing council of seven but was not for a time permitted to serve, perhaps because of insubordination. Settlement made at Jamestown; Smith made notes about events. In September, made supply officer. Captured by the Indians.

1608   Taken to Powhatan, leader of Virginia Indians, and rescued from death, according to Smith's account, by Pocahontas, Powhatan's daughter. Made Powhatan's son and named Nantaquas. In May, sent to England an account of happenings in Virginia, which later in year was published as *A True Relation.* Explored Chesapeake Bay and the Potomac River. Elected president by the governing council. In December, sent to London a map and a description of the area, which after revision was published as part of *A Map of Virginia* (1612).

1609   Badly burned in a powder explosion; returned to England in October.

1610–1611   Worked on material published in *A Map of Virginia.*

1612   Publication of *A Map of Virginia.*

1614   Sailed for America in March; arrived at Maine in late April. Explored Maine and Massachusetts coast. Returned to England in August, with plans for a colony in the area he named New England. Named Admiral of New England by Plymouth Company.

1615   Sailed for America in the spring. When his ship was unable to continue, returned to England and set out in a smaller ship. Soon captured by pirates, who took Smith on board, where he wrote *A Description of New England.* Escaped to France; finally returned to England.

1616   Publication of *A Description of New England.* Visited

	Pocahontas in London. Planned new venture to America.
1617	With three ships prepared to sail to New England. Delayed by winds for three months; expedition canceled.
1618	Requested a financial grant from Lord Bacon to start a colony in New England.
1618–1619	Sought means to return to America.
1620	Publication of *New Englands Trials.*
1622	Enlarged edition published of *New Englands Trials.*
1622	Requested the Virginia Company to send him to Virginia to avenge a massacre.
1623	Published prospectus of *Generall Historie.*
1624	Publication of *Generall Historie.*
1626	Publication of *An Accidence.*
1627	Publication of an enlarged edition of *An Accidence,* entitled *A Sea Grammar.*
1629	Prepared *The True Travels.*
1630	Publication of *The True Travels.*
1631	Publication of *Advertisements for the unexperienced Planters of New England.* Death of John Smith.

CHAPTER *1*

The America of the Elizabethans

C APTAIN JOHN SMITH as adventurer and writer stood in the tradition of the great Elizabethan voyagers. Like them, he sought to extend English power; he delighted in adventures into the unknown; and, like some of them, he provided posterity with reports of his adventures; for, as he wrote in his autobiography, "Many of the most eminent warriors and others, what their swords did, their pens writ" (809). John Smith's life and works are what Irving Story has called them, "a climax to an English sequence extending over half a century."[1] Through Smith America came to share in the tradition of the Elizabethan voyagers; and, to understand Smith, we must first look back to them.

The end of the Elizabethan Age and the early years of the seventeenth century were for England an age of foreign travel, for men's horizons had widened with the discovery of the New World. For England, what has been called "The Age of Drake" began as early as 1562, when John Hawkins transported a cargo of slaves from Africa to the West Indies where he traded them to the Spaniards for sugar, hides, and pearls. Of no great significance in itself, the voyage had important consequences. It offered encouragement to the English to do additional business in the Caribbean, though the Spanish authorities did not welcome Englishmen in what they considered their exclusive territory. When a later voyage by Hawkins led to disaster—the Spaniards nearly destroyed a fleet of six English ships in the West Indies—Francis Drake, who had served with Hawkins, sought to outwit the Spaniards and avenge the loss by raiding the Isthmus of Panama in 1572. Drake seized a rich hoard of precious metals near Nombre de Dios; then, in 1577–80, while circumnavigating the globe, he raided Spanish ports and ships on the coast of Peru.[2]

These events created great excitement in England, for they revealed the riches available in the New World. Earlier, in 1493, Pope Alexander had established the principle that lands discovered not belonging to a Christian prince were the property of the prince under whom the discoveries were made. Shortly thereafter John and Sebastian Cabot's explorations had given England claim to the North American coast from Newfoundland to Florida.[3] England, however, had been too poor to try colonization at that time. By the 1580's, becoming aware of its strength and stability and the riches abroad, England could no longer resist the temptation to establish its own colonies.

I A Colony in Newfoundland

The one part of America well known to Englishmen was the coast of Newfoundland, where the fish caught on the nearby banks were salted and dried. These processes took place only in the late spring and summer, and the winter weather was unknown. If a colony were to be established in Newfoundland, it was thought, fishing might be more profitable: salt could be made there, and drying apparatus could be kept ready for use. It was believed that food was readily available, as well as iron, copper, and timber.

The patent for colonization of the area was held by Sir Humphrey Gilbert from 1578 to 1584; and, though he was more interested at first in piracy than colonies, he finally planned a settlement. After mustering funds from Sir Philip Sidney, among others, he sailed in June, 1583, for Newfoundland with five ships and two hundred and sixty men. Though the largest ship, supplied by Sir Walter Raleigh, soon deserted, the remaining voyagers crossed the seas and established themselves. But, in their efforts to extend their claim, they ran into bad weather, one ship hit a shoal, and nearly all of the men who were to have been colonists were drowned. Gilbert, who headed back to England, was determined, however, to try again in the spring. But near the Azores the remaining ships hit rough water, and Gilbert and his ship went down. Despite this disaster, a very favorable—indeed, eloquent—report of the expedition was prepared by Edward Haie, captain of a surviving ship, who was very optimistic about the commodities of Newfoundland:[4]

We could not observe [wrote Haie] the hundredth part of creatures in those uninhabited lands, but these mentioned [Haie's catalogue occupies two pages] may induce us to glorify the magnificent God, who hath superabundantly replenished the earth with creatures serving for the use of man, though man hath not used a fifth part of the same, which the more doth aggravate the fault and foolish sloth in many of our nation, choosing rather to live indirectly, and very miserably to live and die within this realm pestered with inhabitants, than to adventure, as becometh men, to obtain an habitation in those remote lands in which nature very prodigally doth minister unto men's endeavors, and for art to work upon. (60)

II Richard Hakluyt

Haie's account was published by Richard Hakluyt (1552–1616), a clergyman with whose work English interest in colonization is intimately connected.[5] At Oxford University, where he had been a student, Hakluyt during the years 1577–82 read whatever he could locate, in ancient and modern languages, concerning discoveries and voyages. As lecturer on cosmology at Oxford, he found himself seeking out sea captains and merchants for more information. He corresponded with Gerhardus Mercator, probably the leading geographer of all Europe. In 1580 Hakluyt began the work for which he was to become famous: he published two narratives by Jacques Cartier on the discovery of the Saint Lawrence River. (Hakluyt had the translation made by the great John Florio, later the translator of Montaigne.) The preface expressed the hope that the work might induce Englishmen to establish a colony in America. Much more important was Hakluyt's publication in 1582 of *Divers Voyages touching the discovery of America.* In it he attempted to establish, through reports of the Cabot discoveries, the English title to North America. He also collected French and Italian documents which supplied information about America, and he prepared an extended list of American commodities and a discussion of the Northwest Passage.

Later Hakluyt composed two other influential works. The first was *A Particular Discourse on the Western Planting* (1584). Intended to induce Elizabeth to plant colonies in America, it set forth a colonial policy based on economic needs, provided an augmented list of the supposed riches of America, and offered a program for colonization.[6] If its influence on Queen Elizabeth was slight, it had its effect; it was read by men such as Sir Walter Raleigh.[7] It has been called "the classic statement of the case for English colonization." But Hakluyt's great work came a few years later. *The Principall Navigations, Voiages and Discoveries of the English Nation* (1589; revised and enlarged, 1598–1600) fills eleven volumes in a modern reprint. Hakluyt's documents reported on far more than travel to America: they treat the Near and Middle East, Africa, and Russia. They include reprints from older books, reports written at Hakluyt's request, materials from his own notes, translations, and captured foreign documents. The influence of Hakluyt is perhaps best suggested by Michael Drayton's ode "To the Virginian Voyage," written in 1606, just before the Jamestown colonists set out. The ode begins:

> You brave heroic minds
> Worthy your country's name,
> That honor still pursue,
> Go, and subdue,
> Whilst loit'ring hinds
> Lurk here at home, with shame.

It ends:

> Thy voyages attend,
> Industrious Hakluyt,
> Whose reading shall enflame
> Men to seek fame,
> And much commend
> To after times thy wit.

Of Hakluyt's work, A. L. Rowse has written, " . . . the focusing of the nation's interest upon America . . . was largely due to the life's work of the younger Richard Hakluyt: it has been given to few men to fertilise the history of their country so prodigiously."[9] Hakluyt also gave England preeminence in the publication of accounts of voyages and travels.

III Motives for Colonization

English motives for colonization were many. Louis B. Wright cites five: (1) the desire to convert the Indians to Protestant Christianity (the Spanish effort to convert the Indians was considered highly undesirable); (2) the expectation of riches, such as the English had captured from the Spanish colonies; (3) the need to establish new markets; (4) the attraction of exotic fruits, herbs, gums, drugs, and other raw materials; and (5) the patriotic desire for an English empire.[10]

Specifically, the English were attracted to North America—or Virginia, as they then called the whole area north of Florida—because of the Cabot voyages, because there they might find the Northwest Passage to Cathay, because the temperate zone would supply a market for woolens, and because the Spaniards and Portuguese had effectively sealed off Central and South America.[11] The fact that they were mostly interested in the North did not preclude the English from expecting riches of the sort that the Spaniards had found in the South. As E. G. R. Taylor put it, " . . . overseas lands spelt mines of gold and silver, markets where silks and spices could be purchased for a song, or failing these, such lands were dismissed as savage and hideous wastes, not worth a moment's consideration."[12]

English efforts to discover a Northwest Passage, though futile, played a role in the story of English colonization overseas; for English exploration in the Northwest, especially that of Martin Frobisher, suceeded (in James A. Williamson's words) in convincing "the English that their seamen were equal to the hardest test that the world could offer, and yielded some part of that immeasurable confidence that the ocean was their field of fame."[13] Colonies were naturally associated with this conviction. The defeat of the Spanish Armada in 1588 also developed English self-confidence.

IV The Roanoke Colony

After Gilbert's effort of 1583, the attempt of Sir Walter Raleigh in the 1580's to establish a permanent colony at Roanoke in what is now North Carolina led to the publication of a work which did something to satisfy the developing English appetite for accounts of the strange new worlds to the west.[14] The book is Thomas Hariot's *A brief and true report of the new found land of Virginia* (1588),[15] which David B. Quinn calls "the most delectable of Americana."[16] The year after its original publication it appeared in Hakluyt's *Principal Navigation,* and in 1590 Theodore de Bry published a multilingual edition (English, Latin, French, and German), embellished with engravings of Indians after drawings by John White, who, like Hariot, had spent a year (June, 1585-June, 1586) at Roanoke.[17] It had seventeen printings in the next twenty-five years and was considered "the leading, the most scientific, authority for the best part of a century."[18]

Hariot's book is both a propaganda tract and a report on the colonists' year in America. He was in an excellent position to write the book, since he had been trained as a scientist and in North Carolina had had special responsibilities for studying the Indians, for making maps of the settlement area, and for surveying the natural resources. As a result, Hariot had a collection of notes when he returned to England and could prepare his report with dispatch. Since Hariot's book is often compared with John Smith's portion of *A Map of Virginia,* it is well to note the differing circumstances of the composition of the two: Smith prepared his book without benefit of notes several years after his Virginia adventures.

Hariot's *A brief and true report* consists of a series of encyclopedia-like discussions of materials readily available for export, foodstuffs, and other commodities useful to colonists; and a long description of the Indians closes the work. Hariot throughout emphasizes the potential of the colony, which he believed to be immense. Of particular interest is his report on a product still important to the area, an herb "called by the inhabitants *uppowac.*"

In the West Indies it hath diverse names, according to the several places and countries where it groweth and is used. The Spaniards generally call it tobacco. The leaves thereof being dried and brought into powder, they use to take the fume or smoke thereof by sucking it, through pipes made of clay, into their stomach and head, from whence it purgeth superfluous phlegm and other gross humors, openeth all the pores and passages of the body. By which means the use thereof not only preserveth the body from obstructions but also if any be, so that they have not been of too long continuance, in short time breaketh them. Whereby their bodies are notably preserved in health and know not many grievous diseases wherewithall we in England are oftentimes afflicted.

This *uppowac* is of so precious estimation amongst them that they think their gods marvelously delighted therewith. ... We ourselves during the time we were there used to suck it after their manner, as also since our return, and have found many rare and wonderful experiments of the virtues thereof, of which the relation would require a volume of itself. The use of it by so many of late, men and women of great calling as else and some learned physicians also is sufficient witness. (344–46)

Hariot was convinced that North Carolina was an excellent site for a permanent colony. He liked the climate and the fertility of the soil, and he admired Sir Walter Raleigh's generosity: Raleigh would grant "five hundred acres to a man only for the adventure of his person" (385). He saw no difficulties which would prevent the establishment of a prosperous colony. The Indians, he reported, "are not to be feared, but they shall have cause both to fear and love us that shall inhabit with them" (368).

Though unrealistic in their optimism, Hariot's comments about the Indians are generally well informed, for he seems to have developed a good acquaintance with their language. He frequently provided Indian names for what he described, and he may have prepared a dictionary of Indian words.[19] Quite possibly he shared some of his knowledge with Captain John Smith, who showed in Virginia a good deal of insight into Indian language and behavior. Hariot's discovery that the Indians were fascinated with scientific and mechanical devices, such as guns and burning glasses, may also have been useful to Smith. The Indians seem to have viewed these devices in much the same light as the Bible, introduced without much effect by the earnest missionary Hariot.

All were regarded as miraculous. *A brief and true report* is so attractive and valuable that it is a pity that the chronicle of the expedition mentioned by Hariot (387) is not extant. An account prepared by the governor of the Roanoke Colony, Ralph Lane, and published by Hakluyt in 1589, is much less significant than Hariot's work.[20]

V Raleigh and Guiana

The Roanoke colony's failure resulted from the intervening war with Spain in 1588 and from a lack of long-range planning and substantial investment. Raleigh was interested in quick returns, and Spain was almost an obsession with him. He was determined that England should not be second to her dreaded enemy; and, since he believed the key to Spain's power to be the gold which her South American colonies provided, he wanted to obtain comparable wealth for England. He began, therefore, to collect information about Spanish explorations in South America; and he soon began to focus on Guiana. Hakluyt had observed in 1582 in his *Discourse of Western Planting* that Europeans had not yet taken over Guiana; but the report was that Guiana might be the location of the famous "El Dorado."

Students of American literature know of "El Dorado" as the legendary land sought by Edgar Allan Poe's gallant knight, but the legend has a basis in history. At the sacred lake of Guatavita in the uplands of Bogotá, the Indian chief performed a solemn religious ceremony of sacrifice each year until the Indians lost their independence. First, the chief anointed his body with oil; then he rubbed it over with gold dust. In this gilded appearance he traveled to the center of the lake by canoe, sacrificed offerings of gold and other precious objects to the lake, and finally jumped into the water and bathed. The story of the gilded man ("el hombre dorado" or "el dorado") and his rich empire spread, but its exact location was lost.[21]

Raleigh believed that Guiana was "a country that hath yet her maidenhead, never sacked, turned, nor wrought. . . . "[22] Since English ships had frequently visited Trinidad, which was an appropriate base for operations, Guiana seemed accessible; and in 1594 Raleigh had need of a means of solving his problems. He had lost his standing with Queen Elizabeth in 1592 when he had married Elizabeth Throckmorton, a maid of honor at court. He had even been imprisoned for a time, and his finances were not what he wanted them to be. To redeem himself, he later wrote,

I did even in the winter of my life [he was about forty but men lived shorter lives in those days] undertake these travels, fitter for boys blasted with misfortune, for men of greater ability, and for minds of better encouragement, that thereby, if it were possible, I might recover but the moderation of excess and the least taste of the greatest plenty formerly possessed. If I had known other way to win, if I had imagined how greater adventures might have regained, if I could conceive what farther means I might yet use, but even to appease such powerful displeasure, I would not doubt but for one year to hold fast my soul in my teeth, till it were performed. (3–4)

So Raleigh went to Guiana. He was away from England less than eight months; and, when he returned, some even doubted that he had made the trip. To remove these doubts and to persuade the Queen to invest in other adventures in Guiana, Raleigh wrote *The Discoverie of the large and bewtiful Empire of Guiana*, which was so popular that it required four editions in 1596. (It was later reprinted by Hakluyt.) Though Raleigh, in fact, had discovered nothing, the area having been explored earlier by the Spaniards, his book is one of the masterpieces of Elizabethan travel writing.

While Raleigh's aim throughout the work was propaganda, he clearly had persuaded himself that the area was capable of supplying England with immense wealth. The country, he reported,

hath more abundance of gold than any part of Peru, and as many or more great cities than ever Peru had when it flourished most. It is governed by the same laws, and the emperor and people observe the same religion and the same form and policies in government as was used in Peru, not differing in any part, and I have been assured by such of the Spaniards as have seen Manoa, the imperial city of Guiana, that for greatness, for the riches, and for the excellent seat, it far exceedeth any of the world, at least so much of the world as is known to the Spanish nation. It is founded upon a lake of salt water of 200 leagues long, like unto *mare caspium*. (17)

In *The Discoverie of Guiana* Raleigh prefaced his own story with an extended history of Spanish activities in the Orinocco River area as a kind of foreword to his own history. Despite his tough-mindedness and skepticism,[23] Raleigh accepted the existence of Amazons "not far from Guiana," whose queens each April met with kings of adjacent countries for sexual intercourse. The daughters so conceived were retained by the Amazons, while the sons were handed on to their fathers (26–27). With similar naïveté he told of being given for food an armadillo, "all barred over with small plates somewhat like to a renocero, with a white horn grow-

ing in his hinder parts, as big as a great hunting horn, which they
use instead of a trumpet. Monardus[24] writeth that a little of the
powder of that horn put into the ear cureth deafness" (50–51).

Raleigh and his men first established a base on the southwest
corner of Trinidad. After having the good fortune to capture Fernando de Berrio, the chief Spanish explorer of Guiana, they prepared vessels for the trip up the Orinoco. They crossed to the
mainland, a distance about the width of the English Channel,
traveled through the delta, then reached the savannah country,
and finally the main stream of the Orinoco. Raleigh found the
country astonishingly attractive: " . . . we passed the most beautiful country that ever mine eyes beheld, and whereas all that we
had seen before was nothing but woods, prickles, bushes, and
thorns, here we beheld plains of twenty miles in length, the grass
short and green, and in divers parts groves of trees by themselves,
as if they had been by all the art and labor in the world so made
of purpose. And still as we rowed, the deer came down feeding by
the water's side, as if they had been used to a keeper's call" (42).
C. S. Lewis called the description "enchanting," and Raleigh's
work as a whole he found to possess "almost every charm that a
prose narrative could."[25]

The English were careful to treat the Indians with special care,
Raleigh reported, for they hoped to make them allies against the
Spaniards, whose treatment of the Indians was infamous. Raleigh
wrote with pride of the care given Indian women by the men of
his company. The passage is unusual since the sexual relations of
English and Indians are seldom discussed in the travel literature
of this period. Raleigh protested "before the majesty of the living
God that I neither know nor believe that any of our company one
or other, by violence or otherwise, ever knew any of their women,
and yet we saw many hundreds and had many in our power, and
of those very young and excellently favored, which came among
us without deceit, stark naked" (44).

As they sought to continue inland, the explorers were blocked
by a great escarpment. One way to reach the plateau beyond
seemed to be by means of the Caroni River, but the heavy summer rains had increased the size and vigor of the stream so that
it was impossible to go on. Besides, they could see in the distance
ten or twelve waterfalls, "every one as high over the other as a
church tower" (54).

Raleigh's evidence for the area's wealth certainly seems inadequate, and he brought back little of value. He did not have equip-
ment to obtain samples, though he and his men saw "all the hills

with stones of the color of gold and silver" (63). Nevertheless, he could promise that "The common soldier shall here fight for gold and pay himself instead of pence with plates a foot broad, whereas he breaketh his bones in other wars for provan [food] and penury. The commanders and chieftains that shoot at honor and abundance shall find there more rich and beautiful cities, more temples adorned with golden images, more sepulchres filled with treasure than either Cortez found in Mexico or Pizzaro in Peru" (71). Raleigh himself had seen none of these riches.

To demonstrate his intention to return to the area, Raleigh left behind a boy and a man, but lack of any real indications that wealth was available made it impossible for Raleigh to go back. If his book did not have the result which he sought, it did much to increase Englishmen's interest in the worlds beyond the horizon and thus prepared the way for other colonies. (It should be added that Raleigh finally returned to Trinidad in 1618 in a last attempt to re-establish himself with Guianan wealth, but the results were catastrophic. Raleigh's son was killed and his trusted colleague Laurence Keymis, unable to find the mine that he had been telling Raleigh about for twenty-three years, committed suicide in despair. Raleigh's supply of ideas was exhausted. All that remained was the splendid dream which he was able to capture only on paper.)

VI A Visit to Cape Cod

Raleigh's continuing interest in American colonization after his first trip to Guiana is shown by the fact that the next piece of propaganda for colonies was dedicated to Raleigh, who indeed held the patent to the North American coast and was actively concerned to protect it. Entitled *A Brief and True Relation of the Discoverie of the North part of Virginia*, this account is by John Brereton, who had made a voyage with Bartholomew Gosnold, Gabriel Archer, and Bartholomew Gilbert (son of Sir Humphrey) in the spring and early summer of 1602, the year in which the account was published.[26] Brereton's attractive pamphlet is too little known, although a condensed version was published by Captain John Smith in the first book of the *Generall Historie*, and another was prepared by William Strachey for his *Historie of Travell in Virginia Britanica*.

Brereton's voyage, the first by Englishmen to the shores of New England, was inspired by an account of the Narragansett region by Giovanni de Verrazano, published by Hakluyt in 1582. The exploration was expected to serve as a prelude to colonization.

The company first saw land at the rocky coast of what is now southern Maine, where they were met by a group of Indians, some of whom seem to have traded with Spanish fishermen. At any rate, "one of them [was] apparelled with a waistcoat and breeches of black serge, made after our sea fashion, hose and shoes on his feet" (4). But, because of uncertain weather and "no very good harbor," the English decided to head southward. After half a day's sail in a stiff breeze they reached a "mighty headland," which they found to be a peninsula. There the fishing was excellent, with codfish in abundance. (Not noted in Brereton's account was the fact that Captain Gosnold decided to name Cape Cod after the fish they found there.) Sailing round the tip of the cape, they came to several attractive islands. Brereton and some others went ashore on one, which they named Martha's Vineyard for Gosnold's daughter. Brereton's description of the island is almost ecstatic:

The chiefest trees of this island are beeches and cedars, the outward parts all overgrown with low, bushy trees, three or four feet in height, which bear some kind of fruit, as appeared by their blossoms: strawberries, red and white, as sweet and much bigger than ours in England, raspberries, gooseberries, hurtleberries, and such; an incredible store of vines, as well in the woody part of the island, where they run upon every tree, as on the outward parts, that we could not go for treading upon them; also many springs of excellent sweet water, and a great standing lake offereth water near the sea side, an English mile in compass, which is maintained with the springs running exceedingly pleasantly through the woody grounds which are very rocky. Here are also in this island great store of deer, which we saw, and other beasts, as appeared by their tracks, as also divers fowls as cranes, hernshaws, bitterns, geese, mallards, teales, and other fowls, in great plenty; also great store of peas, which grow in certain plots all the island over. (5–6)

Further exploration and investigation in the area quite convinced Brereton that he had found paradise on earth, for, compared with Cape Cod and its islands, "the most fertile part of all England is (of itself) but barren" (7).

The English had no trouble with the Indians, with whom they feasted. The Indians liked all of the white man's food except the mustard, "whereat they made many a sour face" (9). Thereafter the Indians traded freely, and the English received an abundance of furs. When they finally departed, the Indians "made huge cries and shouts of joy unto us, and we, with our trumpet and cornet and casting up our caps into the air, made them the best farewell we could" (10). Though Brereton called the Indians savages, he painted a very attractive picture of them. He credited the climate for both their strength of body and their wit; and he remarked that, even though the English stayed there but a short time, the men "were much fatter and in better health than when we went out of England" (11).

The original expectation had been that a group of the voyagers would remain to establish claim to the lands; but, when some of them changed their minds, it was decided that all of the men would be needed for the return trip. Thus the first Englishmen to visit New England left "with as many true sorrowful eyes as were before desirous to see it" (12). They brought back to England a valuable cargo of sassafras roots, then considered medicinal.

The report of Gosnold's voyage by Brereton, who was an Anglican clergyman, was published through the good offices of Richard Hakluyt, who was always looking for propaganda. Other supporting documents were also included in the pamphlet, and in a second edition—indicating that the voyage was of considerable interest—appeared "Inducements to the liking of the voyage intending toward Virginia," another aspect of Hakluyt's continuing campaign to colonize America.

VII A Colony in Maine

Gosnold's voyage and the published report of it did prepare the way for other voyages, an important one being under the command of George Waymouth; it was well reported by James Rosier, who may have been a Roman Catholic priest, in *A True Relation of the most prosperous voyage made this present yeere 1605, by Captaine George Waymouth, in the Discovery of the Land of Virginia* (1605). Rosier's account is a literate, interesting work;[27] but it lacks the excitement and sense of discovery of Brereton's report on Cape Cod. Like Hariot, Rosier had taken careful notes; indeed, he wrote that he had been employed specifically to "make true report of the discovery" (357), and one can see that he did his work well. The publication of his report was delayed for a brief time, he observed, until plans were completed for a colony to be established in the area. (The plans, under Roman Catholic auspices, collapsed as a result of the Gunpowder Plot, late in 1605). Rosier made the location of the site obscure to prevent "some foreign nation, from gaining "some knowledge of the place" (358).

Though Weymouth, the leader of Rosier's company, may have intended to explore the area visited by Gosnold in 1602, winds drove them farther north after they had sighted Nantucket. The area they thus inadvertently visited proved to be as fruitful as the more southern area. Fish were plentiful and the soil was rich. St. George's Harbor, Maine, was not only a "good harbor (which is an excellent comfort) but because every day we did more and more discover the pleasant fruitfulness, insomuch as many of our company wished themselves settled here, not expecting any further hopes or discovery to be made" (366). (Since the company consisted of only twenty-nine, the original intention was to leave just two men behind.) They soon made contact with the Indians, whom they admired for their "exceeding good invention, quick understanding, and ready capacity" (368). While the English feared the Indians' treachery, probably with good reason, the Indians were also dubious about the English, who pretended to be interested only in trading. Having made a great show of friendliness, the English were in a position to take captives, "a matter of great importance for the full accomplishment of our voyage" (379). When they were brought back to England, the Indians' presence stimulated further interest in colonization; it seems to have led to the Jamestown venture.

The English do not seem to have considered this kidnapping cause for the Indians to distrust them, for Rosier reported that "we used the people with as great kindness as we could devise or found them capable of." The reason was self-interest: "we found the land a place answerable to the interest of our discovery, viz, fit for any nation to inhabit" (371).

Much of Rosier's *Relation* is a report on the Indians, for curiosity about them was great. When one of the Englishmen spent a night with them, he was able to describe a religious ceremony he had witnessed. It began when a leader in the midst of a gathering of his people, stood and,

looking about, suddenly cried with a loud voice, "Baugh, Waugh." Then the women fall down and lie upon the ground. And the men all together answering the same, fall a stamping round about the fire with both feet, as hard as they can, making the ground shake, with sundry outcries and change of voice and sound. Many take the fire-sticks and thrust them into the earth, and then rest awhile. Of a sudden beginning as before, they continue stamping till the younger sort fetched from the shore many stones, of which every man took one, and first beat upon them with their fire-sticks, then with the stones beat the earth with all their strength. (374)

The cry "Baugh, Waugh," or rather *pow-wow*, came to be a name used to refer to such ceremonies.

Rosier's work is full of notes intended to demonstrate the usefulness of the area as a site for a colony. Particularly attractive to the explorers was the aforementioned St. George's River, which they considered incomparable, finer than the Orinoco, according to some of the party who had seen it with Sir Walter Raleigh. The St. George was "the most rich, beautiful, large, and secure-harboring river the world affordeth" (384). Even hunger could not keep the explorers from continuing up the river, not because they needed to know more about it but because they could not deny themselves the pleasure of seeing its beauty. Like Brereton and later Captain John Smith, Rosier saw New England at its summer best. Those who spent a winter there had a different story to tell.

This voyage, Rosier's account, and the five Indians whom the explorers brought back with them from what is now Maine created such interest in a settlement in the north of "Virginia" that at last one was attempted: Sir John Popham and Sir Ferdinando Gorges planned a permanent colony in Maine on the Sagadahoc River. (Raleigh had now lost his rights in North America.) Though a substantial group of colonists was sent out in 1607, six months after the Jamestown settlers had left, the Northern group found the Maine winter too severe and returned to England in 1608.[28]

VIII William Strachey

One of the best reports of a voyage to America from a literary point of view was written by William Strachey, who was bound for Virginia in 1609 when his ship, carrying Sir Thomas Gates and Sir George Somers, was wrecked in the Bermudas. Gates was on his way to be successor to Captain John Smith as governor of the Virginia colony; Somers was admiral of a flotilla of seven ships and two pinnaces, carrying six hundred colonists. Those who were not shipwrecked and went on to Virginia were less fortunate than Strachey's party, for few survived the difficult winter in Virginia.

A True Reportory of the Wrack and Redemption of Sir Thomas Gates, Knight, upon and from the Islands of the Bermudas is an extended account of the Bermuda and Virginia adventures by a man who served as secretary of the Virginia colony's governing council.[29] Later Strachey also wrote *The Historie of Travell into Virginia Britania.* Neither work was published in his lifetime— the latter, indeed, not until the nineteenth century. *A True Reportory* was first published in 1625, when it appeared in *Purchas His Pilgrimes.* It seems, however, to have circulated widely before that time in manuscript, as is evidenced by the fact that William Shakespeare drew on it for the writing of *The Tempest.*[30] What interested Shakespeare was Strachey's description of the storm which led to the wreck. Another admirer was the nineteenth-century critic Moses Coit Tyler, who found that some sentences in it, "for imagination and pathetic beauty, for vivid implications of appalling danger and disaster, can hardly be surpassed in the whole range of English prose."[31]

Strachey's ship had begun to leak badly at the very beginning of the storm, and much of the description deals with the efforts to locate the leak and prevent the ship from sinking:

... there might be seen master, master's mate, boatswain, quartermaster, coopers, carpenters, and who not, with candles in their hands, creeping along the ribs viewing the sides, searching every corner, and listening in every place if they could hear the water run. Many a weeping leak was this way found and hastily stopped, and at length one in the gunner room made up with I know not how many pieces of beef. But all was to no purpose; the leak (if it were but one) which drunk in our greatest seas and took our destruction fastest could not then be found, nor ever was, by any labor, counsel, or search. The waters still increasing and the pumps going, which at length choken with bringing up whole and continual biscuit (and indeed all we had, ten thousand weight), it was conceived as most likely that the leak might be sprung in the bread room; whereupon the carpenter went down and ripped up all the room but could not find it so. (8–9)

In the meanwhile, "It could not be said to rain; the waters like whole rivers did flood in the air" (7). The wind blew the ship "at all adventurers, sometimes north and northeast, then north and by west, and in an instant again varying two or three points, and sometimes half the compass" (13).

At last Somers saw land, after four days and three nights of storm, but the land was the infamous Devils' Islands, believed to be "no habitation for men but rather given over to devils and wicked spirits" (16). Though Strachey found the islands pleasanter than their reputation suggested, he was much less impressed with this uninhabited area than had been the English who had inspected North Carolina, Guiana, Cape Cod, Maine, and Virginia. Presumably, the frustration of being unable to get to Virginia, his destination, made him blind to the many virtues of the islands. (In 1613 William Crashaw wrote that the landing at the Bermudas was the work of God, who meant this paradise for the English.[32]) Strachey fairly reported, however, the rich supply of food which the islands provided: fish, fowl, wild hogs, turtles ("reasonable toothsome"); but the weather was unpleasant, especially the winter, which was "heavy and melancholy" (21).

Having built a ship, the *Deliverance,* Somers and his men found their way to Jamestown, where they discovered immense "wants and wretchedness" (67) among the colonists, despite the richness of the land. New arrivals and those who had survived the winter all felt that they had no choice but to abandon Virginia. They made plans to leave when reinforcements and supplies arrived. Strachey ended his *Reportory* with a brief account of life in Jamestown and recent events there.

Strachey's longer work, *The Historie of Travell into Virginia Britania,* was written between about 1609 and 1612, though not published until 1849.[33] It is much like Smith's *Generall Historie* in that it is largely a compilation of other men's writings, with some additions based on the author's experiences in Virginia. Strachey made extensive use of Smith's portion of *A Map of Virginia;* in fact, he borrowed about four-fifths of it, without indicating—as Smith usually did—the fact that he was borrowing.

Despite the similarity noted, Smith's and Strachey's books are very different. Strachey had studied at Cambridge University and was friendly with London members of the literary profession. Smith was much less well educated and was a soldier by profession. Something of Strachey's learning and art can be seen in the prefatory paragraph to his first chapter on the Indians:

It were not perhaps too curious a thing to demand how these people might come first, and from who, and whence, to inhabit these so far remote westerly parts of the world, having no intercourse with Asia, Africa, nor Europe, and considering the whole world, so many years, by all knowledge received, was supposed to be only contained and circumscribed in the discovered and travelled bounds of those three, according to that old conclusion in the schools, "Quicquid praeter Africam, et Europam est, Asia est." Whatsoever land doth neither appertain unto Africa nor to Europe is part of Asia. As also to question how it should be, that they, if descended from the people of the first creation, should maintain so general and gross a defection from true knowledge of God, with one kind, as it were, of rude and savage life, customs, manners, and religion, it being to be granted that with us (infallibly) they had one and the same descent and beginning from the universal deluge, in the scattering of Noah's children and nephews with their families (as little colonies) some to one, some to other borders of the earth to dwell. (53)

Unfortunately Strachey did not write a history of the Virginia colony during the years 1609–11, when he was there; in fact, the *Reportory* provides more information about events in Virginia than does the *Historie.* Instead, in preparing the *Historie,* Strachey supplemented Smith's reports on the land and its people. His borrowings from Smith begin with the very first paragraph of the *Historie:*

Smith	Strachey
Virginia is a	Virginia Britania is a
country in America that	country in America that
lieth between the degrees of	lieth between the degrees of
34 and 44 of the north	30 and 44 of the north
latitude, the bounds thereof	latitude, the bounds whereof
on the	must be thus laid: on the
east side are the great	east runneth the great
ocean.	ocean or main Atlantic sea;
On the south lieth Florida;	on the south lieth Florida;
on the north, Nova Francia.	on the north, Nova Francia.
As for the west thereof, the	As for the west thereof, the
limits are unknown. Of all	limits are unknown, only it
this country we purpose not	is supposed there may be
to speak, but only of that	found the descent into the
part which was planted by	South Sea, by the Spaniards
the Englishmen in the year of	called Mar del sur, so
our Lord 1606. (47)	meeting on the backside (as it were)
	of us with that doubtful Northwest
	Passage which leads into the east to
	China, Cathay, Japan. ... (31)

Borrowing such as this by a writer as talented as Strachey strikes one as strange indeed.

Strachey's work is a fragment, perhaps because his efforts at publication received no encouragement. What he left is valuable, though it is not what the title suggests, a history of Virginia. The *Historie* is in two books. The first is devoted to a description of Virginia and its people; the second begins the story of voyages to America but gets no farther than the story of the colony at Sagadoc. Since Strachey did not have it published, the *Historie* did not contribute to interest in Virginia, but its format is helpful in understanding the similar shape of Smith's *Generall Historie.*

IX Hakluyt and Purchas

While Virginia's indebtedness to Richard Hakluyt is not fully known, that propagandist for colonization was probably more responsible than any other man for the continuing interest in colonies. It is natural to find him among the patentees of the London Virginia Company in 1606. He seems to have been expected to serve the colony as chaplain, but perhaps he was too old to make the trip. In the critical year 1609, when the colony was in desperate straits, he translated from the Portuguese an account of De

Soto's explorations in southeastern North America. Entitled *Virginia Richly Valued by the description of the mainland of Florida her next neighbor*, the work was dedicated to the Virginia Company: the book was said to "yield much light to our enterprise now on foot." Hakluyt also published *Nova Francia, or the description of that part of New France which is one continent with Virginia* (1609), which was expected to provide "greater encouragement . . . to prosecute that generous and goodly action," the colonizing of America, according to the preface.[34] Again publication was connected with colonization.

Hakluyt's work was carried on by a successor, a man whose career and that of John Smith touched at several points. According to E. G. R. Taylor, Smith was Samuel Purchas's most important friend.[35] Purchas was like Hakluyt, a clergyman and began his publishing career in 1613, when a substantial folio volume appeared entitled *Purchas His Pilgrimage*, a history of religion with considerable emphasis on geography. Purchas found the collections of Hakluyt particularly useful, as he acknowledged; and, as a result, Hakluyt supplied him with manuscripts which he used in the second edition of the *Pilgrimage* in 1614.

After Hakluyt's death, Purchas obtained (on "hard conditions," he noted) Hakluyt's papers. With them and his own collections he prepared *Hakluytus Posthumus, or Purchas His Pilgrimes*. (The *Pilgrimes* is sometimes confused with the earlier *Pilgrimage*.) Though Purchas was the successor to Hakluyt, his work was distinctly different from that of the great Elizabethan. Hakluyt was a collector of documents which he had sought out or had prepared: he compiled archives. Purchas's work is a history of travel and exploration, portions of which are documents and accounts, usually in abridged form or excerpted.[36] Purchas wanted to provide a readable book. (He was doubtless influenced by the fact that King James had read the *Pilgrimage* seven times). He avoided all that he considered tedious; and, though historians are appalled by the editing which was a consequence, Samuel Taylor Coleridge in "Kubla Khan" shows that the book long retained its attractiveness.[37] (Coleridge, it will be recalled, was reading *Purchas* one day in 1797 when he fell asleep; when he awoke, he found that the poem "Kubla Khan" wrote itself.) Like Hakluyt, Purchas was a propagandist for American colonization; he considered it a work pleasing to God. Perhaps here one can find an adumbration of the concept of America's manifest destiny.

Purchas and Captain John Smith may well have known each other before Smith went to Virginia, and Smith assisted in the preparation of the *Pilgrimage* of 1613. Purchas in turn helped Smith in the preparation of the *Generall Historie* by permitting him to use materials which were to be used in the *Pilgrimes*.[38] Hakluyt's and Purchas's works also served as models for Smith in the preparation of his *Generall Historie*. One other aspect of the relationship should be mentioned: Smith provided an account of his own travels in Hungary and Russia for the *Pilgrimes*.

Travel, discovery, reports, propaganda, and colonization are closely connected in the story of Englishmen in the days of Elizabeth I and James I. It was not enough for men to discover virgin lands across the sea. It took the writings of men such as Hakluyt, Hariot, Raleigh, and Smith to inspire men with a vision of these lands and of the possibilities that awaited them there. This literature of travel and exploration had a tremendous impact on England and, indeed, the world. If the discovery of the New World was the most important event in the history of the Old, the reason was to a considerable extent this literature and its fruits. The promotion pamphlet in particular is, as Louis B. Wright states, "a form of literature not often noted by critics but perhaps of greater significance than poetry or the novel upon the quality of our civilization. . . . "[39]

CHAPTER 2

The Place of Writing in the Life of Captain John Smith

J OHN SMITH'S published writings are eight in number; a modern edition fills two substantial volumes. But only one of the eight can really be regarded as a book. Four are pamphlets of less than fifty pages, one of them, the first version of *New Englands Trials*, being a mere twenty pages. *A Map of Virginia* is indeed a small book, but Smith's contribution constitutes only the first third, less than forty pages.

Furthermore, Smith's one real book, the *Generall Historie*, includes a reprinting, with only small changes and additions, of his portion of *A Map of Virginia* (Book II), his *Description of New England*, and his *New Englands Trials* (Book VI)—in all, about a fifth of the whole. Of the remainder of the *Historie*, little is new. Book I is a collection of travel accounts edited by Smith, Book IV is mostly compilation, and Book V is a history of Bermuda compiled mostly from one source. Even the most famous portion of the *Generall Historie*, Book III, the story of Smith's adventures in Virginia, is a revision of the account published in *A Map of Virginia*, a report in which Smith's contribution was slight. Smith did indeed add to Book III a good many pages, including a few which tell the familiar story of his rescue by Pocahontas. The *Generall Historie* was for two hundred years and more of real value as a compilation made by a knowledgeable authority. It contains occasional fresh pages of comment and historical writing, but it is scarcely an original work.

Nevertheless, the preparation of the *Historie* took time and effort, perhaps a year and a half. In contrast, *A Description of New England* was written in 1615 while Smith was captive aboard the *Don de Dieu*, a French corsair.

I   Facts of Publication

Smith had begun his writing career fortuitously, for his first publication, *A True Relation* (1608), was a letter written to an acquaintance in England; it was definitely not intended for publication. His second work might be called an occasional piece, for

A Map of Virginia (1612) was intended to counteract what Smith and his friends considered to be false reports. Although with *A Description of New England* (1616) Smith seems to have found his proper medium, a mixture of reporting and propaganda, in the next few years he wrote only one other work of this sort, *New Englands Trials* (1620; enlarged 1622). Two of his last works give the impression of having been written for profit: *An Accidence* (1627); and the *True Travels* (1630), an account of Smith's pre-Virginia adventures, published in part by Samuel Purchas in 1625. *Advertisements For the unexperienced Planters* (1631), one of Smith's most impressive works, is a kind of valediction, though in it he wrote that he was then working on a history of the sea. Presumably he did not finish it; it is not extant.

These facts of publication suggest that Smith was a man who turned to writing only from time to time, except for the period when he prepared the *Generall Historie.* What Smith otherwise did in the years between 1617, when he found frustration in what appear to be his final plans to return to America (he did not stop hoping to go), and his death in 1631, is known only hazily. His biographers have pieced together what little information there is, mostly concerning the circumstances surrounding the publication of his work and his known associates in these last years. But the account of these fourteen years fills only fifty-eight pages of Barbour's authoritative biography, and much of the material is tangential. A little more information has recently come to light from the discovery of complimentary poems published in the books of other writers. They underscore what similar poems in Smith's works indicate: that he had a good many literary acquaintances. One seems to have been John Donne, who wrote a poem for the *Generall Historie;* another was John Taylor, the water poet, for whose *Armado* (1627) Smith wrote a poem. (Smith calls Taylor his friend, and Donne calls Smith the same.) The place of writing in Smith's life would be easier to ascertain if more were known about these last years. Very little is known, for example, about the circumstances surrounding the composition of *The True Travels.* From what facts are available about Smith's life it is clear that writing was, as Bradford Smith put it, "not his life but a substitute for living."[1]

II Who Touches This Book, Touches a Man

Until 1617, when he was thirty-seven, Smith's life had been very full. He had been a soldier in the Netherlands and in Hungary; he had toured France, Italy, the Mediterranean, Russia, Central Europe, and North Africa; he had been enslaved in Turkey and Tartary—all before he was twenty-five. As late as 1628 Smith considered himself not a writer but a soldier, as is indicated by his poem on Robert Norton's *The Gunner Shewing the Whole Practice of Artillery:* "We soldiers do embrace/This rare and useful work." (Smith signed the poem "Captain John Smith, Hungarienses.") In the preface to the *Generall Historie* he excuses his writing on the grounds that "The style of a soldier is not elegant but honest and justifiable"(279).

Soon after his return from his foreign adventures, Smith was a participant in the early stages of planning the Virginia colony, was made one of the seven councilors appointed to govern the colony, took a crucial role in the colony's early activities, was made president of the governing council, and was back in England less than three years after he had left. These were the years Smith liked to remember. The years after his return in 1609 through 1617 are less fully known, but much time can be accounted for: preparing two publications; making a trip to New England; making plans for two other trips to America, both of which miscarried. After 1617, he waited impatiently for another chance for adventure.

Because his life was an exciting and frustrating one, Smith's writings reflect in the most direct possible manner his own activities, which pop up in unlikely places, with the result that his writings appear to many readers to be egotistical. Thus *Advertisements for the unexperienced Planters* includes a chapter on "My first voyage to new England, my return, and profit." But Smith justified his personal approach, for he noted in the *Historie,* "But had I not discovered and lived in the most of these parts, I could not possibly have collected the substantial truth from such a number of variable relations ... "(279). He protested that "I am no compiler by hearsay but have been a real actor; I take myself to have a property in them" (275). After 1616, Smith's writings reveal a damaged ego. He found that he could not be objective, for his frustrations were always with him. Thus Smith's life and works are not disparate; his works constantly reflect his life. Since they were interwoven—all of his writings are at least partly autobiographical—the reader of his works and this study will find it useful to have an overview of Smith's life. Particularly important were the Virginia years, to which Smith frequently referrred in his writings.

III   Smith's Early Years

In the late sixteenth century, English society was not static; and John Smith's father, a Lincolnshire farmer, was able to rise significantly in the social scale. By the end of his life, he owned a brick house; and an inventory of his farm animals and household goods listed these as worth seventy-eight pounds, perhaps ten thousand dollars today. The inventory cites, for example:

Item: one feather bed, a bolster, a blanket, a covering, and two pillows.   23 shillings
Item: two pewter candlesticks, for brass candlesticks, three salts, two pewter cups, one tun, and a bowl of pewter, one pewter basin, and a chafing dish   13 shillings, 4 pence[2]

Smith's father owned his own farm and two sizable pieces of land.[3] Had John Smith taken up his father's occupation, he might have been successful enough to claim the title of gentleman.[4] John Smith won the title, or so he claimed, by a more adventurous process. His father could have called himself a yeoman, but in his will he preferrred to name himself as simply a poor tenant of Lord Willoughby, the lord of the manor.[5] With such a background, John Smith was inevitably class-conscious and ambitious.

Smith's education took place in the school of the neighboring town of Alford and later at Louth, not far away, where he was presumably a boarder. In his autobiography, Smith wrote merely that he had been "a scholar in the free schools of Alford and Louth" (821). He must have started school about the age of six and continued until he was fifteen; many students left at that age. The basis of his studies was Latin, with a good deal of emphasis on grammar and later on composition.[6] Very little of this learning shows in his writings. where he carefully avoided any Latin phrases, unlike most writers of the time. (He did show some knowledge of ancient history.)

But "his mind being even then set upon brave adventures" (822), Smith was determined to go to sea. His father, willing for him to leave school, was not willing for him to run off to seek his fortune. Instead, he arranged for him to serve as an apprentice. (Smith's own account of his activities at this time is confused, but the general outline of events can at least be made out.) Off he went to King's Lynn, some sixty-five miles away, to work for Thomas Sendall, a highly successful merchant. The elder Smith presumably felt that his son's zeal for adventure might be satisfied by the thought that eventually he could travel abroad on Sendall's behalf. But the younger Smith insisted on going to sea immediately; and Sendall was unwilling. After his father's death in 1596, the sixteen-year-old abandoned his apprenticeship. Again the facts are unclear, but it was probably at this time that Smith began to be his own master. He went to the Netherlands, where he began his career as a soldier. There he served three or four years. Obviously this was the kind of apprenticeship he preferred.

In 1599 Smith was back in England, ready for more adventures. He managed to be taken on as a servant by Lord Willoughby's younger son, who was about to tour France. Smith got as far as Orleans before he was sent home. Then occurred a minor but characteristic adventure. Smith decided to spend some time in France, where he was befriended by one David Hume, a Scotsman. Hume borrowed money from Smith, who received in return letters recommending him to the court of King James of Scotland. Off he went to seek his fortune there. Though delayed by shipwreck, he found his way to Scotland, but to no avail. Perhaps to get some perspective, Smith returned home. There he read and learned a good deal about horseback riding. His teacher, a descendant of the last Greek emperor of the Eastern Roman Empire,[7] seems to have given him ideas about adventuring to that part of the world. Already, at the age of twenty, Smith was a much traveled, self-reliant soldier of fortune.

Smith's next series of adventures is the subject of his autobiography; they are best treated in connection with that strange book, the *True Travels*. (See Chapter 7.) Here it is enough to say that for four and a half years, Smith toured France, Italy, Greece, the Balkans, Austria, Poland, and Germany; fought in the wars between the Hungarians and the Turks; was captured and sent to Constantinople, then to the Caucasus, where he escaped. Before returning home, he also toured North Africa. He ended these adventures with a name for himself. He had been made captain (and entitled a gentleman) and thus escaped the anonymity of simple John Smith.

IV   Smith in Virginia

By 1605 Smith had by no means satisfied his taste for adventure. He next intended, he later noted, to go to Guiana to join the English colony there: "I should have been a party" (896). Instead, he somehow became identified with a group of men planning a trip to North America to establish a new colony.[8] Smith seems to have known little about the backers of the venture; later, when he was in Virginia and responsible to them, he was extremely unsympathetic with their demands. The men Smith came to know at this time were the leaders of the group who came to America: Captain Bartholomew Gosnold, whose voyage to Cape Cod in 1602 had been attractively written up by John Brereton; Edward Maria Wingfield, a well-born ex-soldier in his forties; and Christopher Newport, a highly experienced seaman who was to conduct the colonists to Virginia and then bring over supplies. Smith probably also talked with Thomas Hariot, who had written about his year with the Roanoke colony in North Carolina. Very little is known about how Smith became identified with the group; he himself explained in 1620 that he had invested over "five hundred pound" in the undertaking (242). (According to one version of his European adventures, he had returned to England with a thousand ducats, about five hundred pounds.[9]) The records indicate that Smith's subscription was nine pounds.

Before the colonists left, they received elaborate instructions from the group that sponsored them, the London Virginia Company. The officers of the colonists carefully followed these instructions, though the consequences were often undesirable. For example, the site of the colony, Jamestown, was an extremely unhealthy place, and many colonists died as a result; but the location was very like what the **instructions** called for. Smith was not happy to be obliged to follow directions prepared by men remote from the place where decisions had to be made, yet he, too, often found that he had no choice but to do so. Among the most important instructions were the following:

> When it shall please God to send you on the coast of Virginia, you shall do your best endeavour to find out a safe port in the entrance of some navigable river, making choice of such a one as runneth farthest into the land, and if you happen to discover divers portable [navigable] rivers, and amongst them any one that hath two main branches, if the difference be not great, make choice of that which bendeth toward the northwest, for that way you shall soonest find the other sea.
>
> . . . .
>
> You must observe if you can whether the river on which you plant doth spring out of mountains or out of lakes. If it be out of any lake, the passage to the other sea will be more easy, and [it] is like enough that out of the same lake you shall find some spring which run the contrary way towards the East India Sea, for the great and famous rivers of Volga, Tanais, and Dwina have three heads near joined, and yet the one falleth into the Caspian Sea, the other into the Euxine Sea, and the third into the Paelonian Sea.
>
> In all your passages, you must have great care not to offend the naturals,

if you can eschew it, and employ some few of your company to trade with
them for corn and other lasting victuals. ... [10]

In December, 1606, a group of a hundred and five colonists
departed in three ships.[11] Of these at least fifty-nine were "gentlemen" who could not be expected to work. They traveled via
the West Indies, where one colonist died from the heat. Smith had
meanwhile been made prisoner, presumably as a result of some
disagreement. Arriving in April, 1607, the colonists were soon
attacked by Indians. They located a site, named it Jamestown, and
began to fortify it. The ruling body was a group of seven men:
Newport; Wingfield, who was elected president; Gosnold; Captain John Martin; Captain George Kendall; Captain John Ratcliffe;
and Captain John Smith, one of the most obscure of the group.
Smith was not for a time, however, permitted to serve; but, when
Captain Newport began an exploration of the James River, as the
"Instructions" required, Smith was a member of the exploring
party. This journey up the James convinced Newport that the
Pacific Ocean was only a little way farther.

Not until June, 1610, was Smith admitted to the council; and by
that time several colonists had been killed by the Indians in both
major attacks and minor skirmishes. Soon after, on June 22, Newport and two ships returned to England, and with him went a
letter from the six remaining members of the council that provides
insight into the situation of the colonists, especially into one of the
most serious problems they faced: the sailors of the supply ships,
always ready for a quick profit, subverted the work of the settlers.
The letter reads, in part:

We have sown a good store of wheat; we have sent you a taste of clapboard
[used for making casks]; we have built some houses; we have spared some
hands to a discovery; and still as God shall enable us with strength we will
better and better our proceedings. Our easiest and richest commodity,
being sassafras roots, were gathered up by the sailors with loss and spoil of
many of our tools and with drawing of our men from our labor to their uses
against our knowledge to our prejudice. We earnestly entreat you and do
trust that you take such order as we be not in thus defrauded, since they
be all our waged men, yet do we wish that they may be reasonably dealt
withall so as all the loss neither fall on us nor them. I believe they have
thereof two tons at the least, which if they scatter abroad at their pleasure
will pull down our price a long time. This we leave to your wisdoms.[12]

Though food was in short supply after the departure of Newport,
the colonists, instead of establishing themselves, did little; and the

leaders disagreed among themselves. Before long, death began to thin out rapidly the ranks of the settlers; Captain Gosnold was among those to die. The troublesome Captain Kendall was removed from the council, reducing the number to four. In September, Wingfield was removed from command and from the council for incompetence by the remaining three, who elected Ratcliffe president. Smith became supply officer.

The adventures of the period from September, 1607, to June, 1608, including encounters with Powhatan, the Indian leader, are described in Smith's *True Relation,* which he wrote at the end of this period. (See Chapter 3.) By June, when Smith sent his *True Relation* to England, Wingfield and Martin had decided to return to home; and Smith's importance in the life of the colony was steadily growing. He led exploring missions on long trips up Chesapeake Bay during the summer; and in September, when Ratcliffe's term expired, Smith was elected president.

Soon he found himself forced to follow new instructions prepared by the London backers of the colony, though they were, from Smith's point of view, very impractical. They included orders to crown Powhatan, an effort to encourage the Indian leader to be more subservient to the English. (The crowning took place but did not have the desired effect.) Smith was also expected to increase the shipment of lumber and other products of the colony to England, though the quantity of supplies coming to the colony from England was minimal, and the visiting sailors continued to create havoc in the colony's economy. Smith's chief problem was to obtain food for the colonists, now two hundred in number. The Indians were the chief source of food, and force increasingly seemed required to obtain it from them. Under Powhatan's leadership, they became more and more pugnacious as a result. At several crucial times, Pocahontas, Powhatan's daughter, came to the aid of Smith and the colonists.

Smith's leadership was having its effects: at last the colonists were put to work. According to the report published as part of *A Map of Virginia,*

Now we so quietly followed our business that in three months, we made three or four lasts of pitch, and tar, and soap ashes; produced a trial of glass; made a well in the fort of excellent sweet water, which till then was wanting; built some twenty houses; recovered our church; provided nets and weirs for fishing; and to stop the disorders of our disorderly thieves, and the savages built a blockhouse in the neck of our isle, kept by a garrison, to entertain the savages' trade, and none to pass or repass, savage or christian, without the president's order. Thirty or forty acres of ground we digged and planted; of three sows in one year increased sixty and odd pigs, and near five hundred chickens brought up themselves, without having any meat given them; but the hogs were transported to Hog Isle, where also we built a blockhouse, with a garrison, to give us any notice of shipping, and for their [the lookouts'] exercise, they made clapboard, wainscot, and cut down trees against the ship's coming. (154)

All seemed to be going well when it was discovered that the grain which was stored for later use had rotted and been eaten by rats. As a result, work was stopped on all these projects; and everyone was set to work finding food. Furthermore, Smith had to struggle with Dutch and Swiss laborers who conspired with Powhatan and the Indians to destroy the colony.

Meanwhile, the Virginia Company had decided to make a larger effort to support and develop the Jamestown colony. Sir Thomas Gates was named head of the colony, to be succeeded later by Lord de la Warr; and a large number of colonists were enrolled. A whole fleet of ships started out for Virginia. But the flagship of the fleet, captained by Newport and with Gates and Sir George Somers—Gates' deputy—aboard, was shipwrecked in the Bermudas. (The shipwreck was vividly described by William Strachey. See Chapter 1.) The remaining colonists arrived in Virginia, and Smith had the responsibility of a command which now was much increased and included many women and children. Because of the food shortage, he broke up the colony into a number of what were supposed to be self-sustaining groups. He also had the additional problem of dealing with the leaders among the recently arrived colonists, some of whom felt that, until Gates arrived, someone else, not Smith, should govern.

Smith was facing the most trying circumstances of his Virginia years. It was early September, and he knew that his days as president were very limited; but much work had to be done before the winter came. He therefore visited the group of colonists who were making a base at the falls of the James River, a hundred miles from Jamestown. Having done what he could for the group, who were on the verge of mutiny, Smith started out for Jamestown. Here is how the 1612 report described what then happened. "[Smith] Sleeping in his boat ... accidentally one fired his powder bag, which tore his flesh from his body and thighs nine or ten inches square, in a most pitiful manner, but to quench the tormenting fire, frying him in his clothes, he leaped over board into the deep river, where ere they could recover him, he was near drowned. In this estate, without either chirurgeon or chirurgery, he was to go near one hundred miles" to Jamestown (165).

Since Smith's accident completely incapacitated him, he left Virginia for England in October, 1609. Though many found fault with his government and sent charges against him back to England, he was much missed by the colonists. Before the winter was over, the misruled colony was barely surviving; and Jamestown would have been abandoned had not Lord de la Warr and fresh supplies arrived. In the winter after Smith left, all but about sixty of the colonists died.

Had Gates and Somers arrived as planned, and Smith not been injured, Captain John Smith would not have continued as president of the council but would have had an important post, that of defense officer of the colony. Later, when he sought to return to Virginia after the Indians had massacred the settlers, it was a military post such as this one that he wanted.

V   Smith and New England

Back in England, Smith found a new friend and supporter in Edward Seymour, Earl of Hertford.[13] Except for this fact, next to nothing is known about the next few years of his life. He prepared a description of Virginia, published in 1612 as part of *A Map of Virginia*, along with a narrative of Virginia events of 1607–10, to which Smith probably contributed. (See Chapter 4.) Meanwhile the Virginia colony was barely surviving. Presumably as a consequence, Smith's attention strayed. He became interested in the area north of Virginia, and in 1614 was given charge of two ships to sail to the Maine coast, often visited by English ships. Smith went there, as he later wrote, "to take whales and make trails of a mine of gold and copper. If those failed, fish and furs was then our refuge, to make ourselves savers however" (187). Smith later told the story of this important voyage in *A Description of New England* (1616). (See Chapter 8.)

After this voyage, Smith met Sir Ferdinando Gorges, an active member of the trading organization known as the Plymouth Company and a sponsor of the Sagadahoc colony, which had wintered on the Maine coast in 1607–1608. According to his 1616 pamphlet, Smith was assured by Gorges "and some others" that he would "have the managing [of] their authority in those parts during my life," and so he engaged himself "to undertake it for them" (219).

Gorges and Smith planned a colony in New England: Gorges with difficulty found the financial support needed, and Smith was to be in charge of a small group of settlers. Two ships set out; but Smith's ship, the larger of the two, soon proved unseaworthy, and he was forced to return to England. Smith started out again in a smaller ship. After a series of misadventures,[14] he found his ship's officers unwilling to continue: they left Smith on a French pirate ship and departed. Only with great difficulty did Smith escape and find his way back to England.[15]

Smith's bad luck must have been obvious to the cautious Gorges, but he had committed himself to Smith, who clearly was experienced with the New World. (This experience was manifested when Pocahontas, now married to John Rolfe, came to England in 1616: Smith reported her good qualities to the Queen.) The persistent Smith finally had another chance to go to America. In the spring of 1617, he was given three ships and a small group of colonists to begin a colony in New England. Smith probably expected to go to Massachusetts, but for three months he and his ships waited wind-bound in Plymouth Harbor. Then, as Smith explained in 1620, "the season being past, the ships went for Newfoundland, whereby my design was frustrate, which was to me and my friends no small loss" (241). This was the last time that Smith began an adventure westward. What connection Smith and Gorges had after this time is not known.

VI   Years of Frustration and Writing

Throughout the remainder of his life Smith tried again and again to find sponsors for a colony in America. He sought support from Lord Bacon in 1618; he published two pleas for support, one in 1620 and another in 1622 (see Chapter 9); and he urged the London guilds to help him. He wanted to guide the Pilgrims, who instead used his book and map on New England. Seeking money in 1621, Smith cited his work for the Jamestown colony; but he again sought in vain. In 1622 he asked the Virginia Company to send him to discipline the Indians.

In the same year, 1622, Captain John Smith began his *Generall Historie.* It was to be a big book, by far Smith's longest. In 1623 he published a prospectus of the work to attract contributors, for printing was to be expensive; and he finally found a sponsor in the widow of the Earl of Hertford, who had aided him more than ten years before. She was now Duchess of Richmond and Lenox, and to her Smith dedicated the *Generall Historie,* published in 1624. (See Chapters 4 and 5.)

In the preparation of his *Historie,* Smith worked with Samuel Purchas, who published a brief account by Smith of his adventures from 1596 to 1604 in *Purchas His Pilgrimes* (1625). (See Chapter 7.) But these last years of Smith's are little known, except for the fact that in 1626 he published, apparently for gain, *An Accidence or the Pathway to Experience,* augmented in 1627 as *A Sea Grammar,* and in 1627 and 1628 he wrote poems of commendation. (See Chapter 6.)

It is known that Smith was keeping alert to developments in America; for, in his continuation to the *Generall Historie,* he reported on what had happened there since 1624. This account appeared in 1630 as the second part of Smith's *True Travels,* the augmented version of his autobiography. Smith's interest in colonies is also shown by his last and best work, *Advertisements for the unexperienced Planters of New England, or anywhere* (1631). (See Chapter 8.) Smith's interest in America still stemmed from his conviction that he was responsible for the existence of the English colonies in America. He explained in the preface to *An Accidence:* "That the most of those fair plantations did spring from the fruits of my adventures and discoveries is evident" (788).

On June 21, 1631, Captain John Smith died, leaving neither wife nor children—except for the American colonies, which were to him both, or so he wrote. His will deeded his Lincolnshire property to Thomas Packer, who in turn was to pay various benefactions. Including the cost of his funeral, these totaled forty pounds. His epitaph was a fitting one.

> Here lies one conquered that hath conquered kings,
> Subdued large territories, and done things
> Which to the world impossible would seem,
> But that the truth is held in more esteem.
>   Shall I report his former service done
> In honor of his God and Christendom?
> How that he did divide from pagans three
> Their heads and lives, types of his chivalry,
> For which great service in that climate done
> Brave Sigismundus (King of Hungarion)
> Did give him as a coat of arms to wear
> Those conquered heads got by his sword and spear?
>   Or shall I tell of his adventures since,
> Done in Virginia, that large continence?
> How that he subdued kings unto his yoke,
> And made those heathen fly, as wind doth smoke,
> And made their land, being of so large a station,
> A habitation for our Christian nation,

Where God is glorified, their wants supplied,
Which else for necessaries might have died?
   But what avails his conquest, now he lies
Interred in earth, a prey for worms and flies?
O may his soul in sweet Elisium sleep,
Until the keeper that all souls doth keep,
Return to judgment, and that after thence,
With angels he may have his recompence. (971–72)

CHAPTER 3

The Reporter

C APTAIN JOHN SMITH provided two kinds of reports on his Virginia years: one narrative, the other expository. He told the story of his first year in Virginia in *A True Relation* (1608), his first book. Though he later added to an account, prepared by others, of the whole of his stay of two and a half years in Virginia, Smith's *True Relation* is the only consecutive report that is wholly his. Since Smith did not prepare it for publication or see it through the press, the book may not be exactly as he wrote it. It has some abruptnesses, such as one just before the final paragraph, that lead one to conjecture that significant omissions were made. Likewise, Smith's second report, a portion of *A Map of Virginia*, is probably not just as he wrote it. In a postscript, the editor of the volume, William Symonds, noted that "The pains I took was great" (174). Nevertheless, these two works are fundamentally Smith's, and they are without question important.

I The First American Book

Histories of American literature traditionally begin with the year 1607, when the Jamestown colony began, or 1608, the date of the first American book. Not written as a book but as a letter to a friend in England, John Smith's *A True Relation of such occurences and accidents of noate as hath hapned in Virginia since the first planting of that Collony* is the first English book written in America. Of course Thomas Hariot's literate and valuable *Brief and True Report* of the Roanoke colony was published in 1588, but it had been written in England, as had the writings on New England of Brereton and Rosier. Other early accounts of Jamestown exist—by Gabriel Archer, George Percy, and Edward Maria Wingfield—but these were not in print as early as Smith's book; two of them, in fact, were not published until the nineteenth century.[1]

II Facts of Publication

A True Relation is a forty-four-page quarto pamphlet, "Written by Captain Smith, Coronell of the said Collony, to a worshipfull friend of his in England"; and its running title is *Newes from*

Virginia. It was written about June 1, 1608, and immediately thereafter sent to England. The unidentified author of the prefatory epistle[2] explained that he came across the letter "by chance (as I take it, at the second or third hand)." (The earliest printing did not identify the author by name, and the second named him as Thomas Watson.) Along with other readers, the author of the preface felt that the letter should be published, "though it cannot be doubted that some faults escaped in the printing, especially in the names of countries, towns, and peoples which are somewhat strange unto us" (3). The writer then explained, tantalizingly, that "somewhat more was ... written" by Smith, "which being as I thought (fit to be private) I would not adventure to make it public" (4). Unlike the rest of Smith's writings published before 1624, *A True Relation* was not revised for republication in *The Generall Historie of Virginia.* After the four printings of 1608, it was not reprinted until the nineteenth century.

A True Relation deals with the events of the first thirteen months of the Jamestown colony, April, 1607–May, 1608. A personal account, a letter, it is not a formal report for posterity, though Smith attempted to provide a fairly full account of the colony's adventures. His own exploits were of considerable importance during the period; and, even if Smith's personal bias is apparent, he was probably in the best position of any of the colonists to write an account. *A True Relation* is the raw material of history, not history itself; for Smith was very close to the events he described. At the beginning of the period with which he dealt, he was a minor figure among the colonists: for some unknown reason, perhaps his insubordination, he was under arrest for the first month or so of the settlement. But, by the end of a year in America, he had demonstrated his worth so effectively that he was soon made president of the governing council.

III Struggles to Survive

These thirteen months were marred by struggles for power, discontent, inertia, near famine, disease, and threats from the Indians. Nevertheless, largely because of Smith's leadership, the colonists did gain some knowledge of their environment. He had been admitted to the governing council in early June, 1607. In his position as supply officer (or cape merchant), a post he was given in September, 1607, he had explored the Chickahominy River, a tributary of the James. He had gone well up the York River, which runs parallel to the James River, a few miles to the north.

Smith had little opportunity to explore merely for the sake of discovery, for the colonists were in desperate need of food. When their ships had left in June, provisions for only thirteen or fourteen weeks were available. The Indians saved the day: when supplies were low, the settlers turned to them for sustenance. With many colonists already dead of famine and disease, Smith describes the situation when he became supply officer, five months after his arrival in America:

At this time were most of our chiefest men either sick or discontented, the rest being in such despair as they would rather starve and rot with idleness than be persuaded to do anything for their own relief without constraint. Our victuals being now within eighteen days spent, and the Indian trade decreasing, I was sent to the mouth of the [James] River to Kecoughtan, an Indian town, to trade for corn and try the river for fish, but our fishing we could not effect by reason of the stormy weather. The Indians, thinking us near famished, with careless kindness offered us little pieces of bread and small handfuls of beans or wheat for a hatchet or a piece of copper. In like manner I entertained their kindness and in like scorn offered them like commodities, but the children or any that showed extraordinary kindness I liberally contented with free gift, such trifles as well contented them. (9)

This early passage from Smith's first work shows the ironic tone which was to become almost characteristic and the awareness of the possibilities of verbal patterns, which unfortunately Smith never developed fully.

IV Captured by Indians

After a number of efforts, Smith was able to accumulate enough corn by bartering to permit him to make a trip mainly for exploration. With a small party of men, he went up the Chickahominy much farther than he had been before, "towards Powhatan," the Indian emperor of whom the colonists had heard soon after their arrival in Virginia. This adventure and Smith's subsequent capture by the Indians are probably the best-known events of his life. The story constitutes nearly a fifth of the *Relation,* but it omitted Smith's memorable rescue by Pocahontas, to which he later frequently referred and which he described vividly in the *Generall Historie.* These facts have made the earlier version less well known and at the same time have, in the judgement of some readers, demonstrated that the rescue in the later version is a fabrication.

Why the two versions differ will never be known. Smith did note in 1608 that "So fat they fed me that I doubted they intended to have sacrificed me to the *Quiyoughquosicke,* which is a superior power they worship" (22); but he described nothing like an execution scene nor did he mention Pocahontas. Bradford Smith, who believed that Pocahontas did at this time rescue Smith, cited several reasons why Smith might have chosen to omit the story in 1608. The most persuasive one is that doing so would have hurt his reputation for bravery and subjected him to "leering remarks about his relations with the girl."[3] Philip Barbour thought that part of the account of Smith's captivity may have been suppressed as a horror story by the man who arranged the printing of the 1608 account. Barbour too accepted the Pocahontas story as true.[4]

Since the trip was the occasion not only of Smith's capture but also of the death of two members of his group, he was quite defensive in his account of the adventure and justified at some length his actions. In all, he listed five factors which led him on when the river had become so narrow that he had had to leave his barge and obtain a canoe to continue: (1) "the friendship of the Indians in conducting me"; (2) "the desolateness of the country," which suggested safety; (3) "the probability of some lake" being just beyond;[5] (4) "the malicious judges of my actions" at Jamestown, who might think him lacking in courage; and (5) the desirability of having "some matter of worth to encourage our adventurers [sponsors] in England" (14).

Exploring on foot, with only an Indian guide with him, Smith found himself surrounded by two hundred men; and, after a fight, he was captured. First brought before the local chieftain, Opechancanough, Smith was paraded through much of the countryside before finally being delivered to Weramocomoco on the Pamunkey (York) River. There, early in January, Smith for the first time saw Powhatan, and what a sight he was

... proudly lying upon a bedstead a foot high, upon ten or twelve mats, richly hung with many chains of great pearls about his neck, and covered with a great covering of rahaughcums [racoon skins]. At [his] head sat a woman, at his feet another; on each side sitting upon a mat upon the ground were ranged his chief men on either side the fire, ten in a rank, and behind them as many young women, each [with] a great chain of white beads over their shoulders, their heads painted in red, and [Powhatan] with such a grave and majestic countenance as drave me into admiration to see such state in a naked savage. (18–19)

This description is remarkably vivid despite the omission of words probably caused by the haste in which Smith was writing—the ship that was to carry his letter to England was ready to weigh anchor. Though the work abounds throughout in slips of many kinds, Smith told his story well and, as in this passage, with an eye for telling detail and an ability to suggest the personality of the narrator and his reaction to what happened.

In his first interview with Powhatan (Smith knew the importance of picking up a working knowledge of a language in a hurry), he was eager to learn all he could of the new land. Powhatan's extended discourse permitted Smith to reply:

I requited his discourse (seeing what pride he had in his great and spacious dominions, seeing that all he knew were under his territories) in describing to him the territories of Europe which was subject to our great king, whose subject I was, the innumerable multitude of his ships; I gave him to understand the noise of trumpets and terrible manner of fighting [of those that] were under Captain Newport my father [the admiral of the fleet that had delivered the colonists], whom I entitled the *Meworames,* which they call the King of All Waters. At his greatness he admired and not a little feared. (20)

This self-possession in the face of danger is characteristic. It was not merely a literary pose; his fellows recognized Smith's virtues, unless the fact that he was a self-made man was found to be offensive. In our age which is not prone to hero worship, Smith's self-portraits may strike readers as phoney; therefore, it is important to remember how those he left behind remembered him when a severe injury forced him to return to England in 1609. The account appears in the narrative portion of *A Map of Virginia* (1612).

. . . thus we lost him that, in all his proceedings, made Justice his first guide and Experience his second, ever hating baseness, sloth, pride, and indignity more than any dangers; that never allowed more for himself than his soldiers with him; that upon no danger would send them where he would not lead them himself; that would never see us want what he either had or could by any means get us; that would rather want than borrow, or starve than not pay; that loved actions more than words and hated falsehood and cozenage worse than death; whose adventures were our lives and whose loss our deaths. (167)

To reject a testimony such as this one takes cynicism, not mere skepticism. Smith later in his career suffered a series of frustrations and, as a consequence, indulged in some very unattractive self-pitying; but, when he had the opportunity to exercise his capacities, he was a highly successful leader and deserves the title of savior of the Jamestown colony.

Smith's coolheadedness enabled him to make many careful mental notes concerning the land which he saw as a captive and the religious ceremonies of his captors. He later set forth these descriptions with care and precision since the geographical information was of obvious value. The facts about the religious life of the Indians might also have proved valuable, or so Smith presumably thought. On the other hand, in view of his very full picture of the culture of the Indians in his portion of *A Map of Virginia*, it is fair to say that this interest shows Smith's love of knowledge for its own sake.

Finally returned by the Indians to Jamestown, Smith had won the friendship of Powhatan: the Indian emperor now sent him supplies once or twice a week. Smith's return pleased some of his jealous colleagues very little: indeed, only the return of Captain Newport and a supply ship saved Smith's life. He was blamed for the deaths of the two men killed by the Indians when he was captured. Once again Smith enjoyed a hairbreadth escape.

V Further Dealings with the Indians

Nearly half of the remainder of *A True Relation* is devoted to Newport's visit, under Smith's supervision, to Powhatan. Though Smith had good reason to suppose that the Indians were now committed to friendship, he was exceedingly wary. Because he knew "by experience the most of their courages to proceed from others' fear" (24), he made something of a display of his own bravery. First, he made a preliminary visit to Powhatan; then he escorted Newport to the Indian leader. Through his narration of this encounter, Smith kept himself in the foreground. It was he who was perpetually on the alert, for he knew that he could believe in Powhatan's friendship only "till convenient opportunity suffered him to betray us" (27). The meetings between the Indians and the English went on for several days during which trading interspersed with "dancing and much mirth." Finally the expedition was completed without loss of life, and food for twelve weeks had been obtained.

Soon after, on April 10, Newport returned to England. (He left none of the food supplies his ship had brought from England, for his crew had eaten them all.[6]) Life at Jamestown settled into a routine not known before. Smith explored the south end of Chesapeake Bay and at Jamestown chastened the Indians, who had been stealing tools in abundance. The arrival in late April of a supply ship with new colonists seemed to permit additional exploration; Smith—above all a military man and always ready for new adventures—and another leader trained a sizable group, including seamen, for six or seven days to prepare them "to march, fight and skirmish in the woods" (34). When his men were ready to start exploring the western reaches beyond the falls of the James River, the plan was vetoed by the ship's captain, who refused to let his men serve without additional pay. Never one to sulk, Smith started the men on tasks at Jamestown. One of the tasks was chopping down trees and preparing lumber for shipment to England; another was planting crops. Smith's official function was still that of supply officer.

The colonists continued to have minor problems with the Indians, who were now plotting to eliminate the English. One plot was revealed when Smith severely frightened a captured Indian, who confessed. In the midst of Smith's not wholly clear account of the Indian-English relations, Pocahontas, Powhatan's daughter, makes her first appearance in Smith's narrative. Her father had sent her, his favorite, to demonstrate—or rather to counterfeit—his affection for Smith. She was "a child of ten years old which not only for feature, counternance, and proportion much exceedeth any of the rest of his people, but for wit and spirit is the nonpareil of his country" (38). (The phrase was to become a favorite with Smith.) We hear no more of Pocahontas in the *Relation*.

Smith's methods of dealing with the Indians were extreme, but they had the effect of establishing an uneasy peace. Thus when an Indian saw that his plan to lead Smith and a group of his men into an ambush was not succeeding and abused the English, Smith "gave him twenty lashes with a rope, and his bow and arrows, bidding him shoot if he durst, and so let him go" (39). (With less severe policies later, one consequence was a massacre of the settlers, or so Smith was to reason.)

VI Smith's Outlook

Smith ended his *Relation* on a thoroughly optimistic note. Crops had been planted; there was no shortage of food. The colonists were even able to ship a load of cedar wood to England on the vessel that carried Smith's letter. Smith concluded with a rhetorical flourish:

We now remaining being in good health, all our men well contented, free from mutinies, in love with one another; and as we hope in continual peace with the Indians, where we doubt not, by God's gracious assistance and the adventurers' willing minds and speedy furtherance to so honorable action, in after times to see our nation to enjoy a country not only exceeding pleasant for habitation but also very profitable for commerce in general, no doubt pleasing to almighty God, honorable to our gracious sovereign, and commodious generally to the whole Kingdom. (40).

After the unpleasant report which Smith provided, this propagandistic conclusion may seem out of place; and Howard Mumford Jones went so far as to suggest that it was not Smith's work.[7] But Smith was consistently optimistic about the possibilities of the New World. From his point of view, most of the troubles which the colonists experienced were due to mistakes, inadequate leadership and supplies, and unwillingness to work hard.

Critics of Smith, such as Alexander Brown, have pointed to his treatment of the leaders of the colony as an example of the bias which they feel vitiates his writings.[8] Smith was highly critical of Captain Edward Maria Wingfield, the first governor, though he wrote little about him. He described his "audacious command." the lack of harmony on the governing council under Wingfield, and his deposition from the presidency in September, when he "was generally hated of all" for the way which he had conducted the colony's affairs (8–9). Smith mentioned other problems of leadership, but on the whole he was not concerned with the leadership or the administration of the colony as much as he was with what was happening. It should not be surprising that his account lacks objectivity, for Smith had a definite point of view—that of a soldier educated chiefly by experience, and of one who was very much a participant in the affairs of the colony.

VII A *True Relation* and American Literature

The first American book is a lively, detailed, personal account of the first permanent English settlement in America. Moses Coit Tyler rightly observed that Smith "wrote a book that is not unworthy to be the beginning of the new English literature in America."[9] It is valuable not only as a historical document or as a landmark in American history but as a work of literature. Its author was a perceptive man as well as a vigorous one. His work has no real structure, for it was written under pressure; but it is not lacking in organization. Instead of composing a chronicle, as many travelers and explorers did, Smith organized much of his material into large blocks, notably those on his capture by the Indians and his visit to Powhatan with Captain Newport. Certain themes tie the work together: the constant danger of attack by the Indians, the lack of knowledge of the area (Chesapeake Bay was largely unexplored, and the falls of the James River had prevented much exploration inland), the increasing importance of Captain John Smith, the outstanding leader of the colony.

H. M. Jones's study of letters and other writing by early Virginia colonists turned up literate prose in surprising quantity, though not many formal literary productions. From his study he was led to conclude that Captain John Smith was not "a sport plant in an unliterary wilderness."[10] Common characteristics were shared by this literature, according to Jones; and some of these prove to be characteristic not only of Smith's earliest work but of all his literary productions. "For this literature," Jones wrote, "the visible world exists. Its writers see and touch and taste and smell. . . . The vast American landscape has laid its spell upon them. . . . "[11] Among the other qualities of this literature noted by Jones are pragmatism, worldliness, unconcern with theology; in sum, it was a "secular literature." The validity of some of Jones's generalizations for Smith's later writings is limited, for Smith did occasionally become introspective and did sometimes indulge in philosophic and moral meditation. But *A True Relation* is otherwise: it is a thoroughly characteristic piece of seventeenth-century Virginia literature.

VIII Back in England

In October, 1609, John Smith was obliged to return to England, after nearly two and a half years in Virginia. He had been badly wounded by a gunpowder explosion, and his year's term as president had expired. He left Virginia with his worst enemies in power. The man appointed to succeed Smith, Sir Thomas Gates, had been shipwrecked in the Bermudas; but the other ships in Gates's fleet had reached Virginia, delivering Captains Gabriel Archer and John Ratcliffe. Both had served with Smith earlier, and there was no love lost among them. These two, with other malcontents, prepared an indictment of Smith; he was to answer charges on his return to London. (There the charges seem to have been largely dropped.) Because of the shipwreck, Smith could not know that the Virginia Company's new orders, which appointed Gates governor, named Smith as second member of the Governor's Council and as defense chief, an appointment demonstrating the confidence the company had in Smith.

Without Smith as leader, the colonists at Jamestown had a difficult time. During the winter following Smith's departure, the "starving time," scarcely sixty of the augmented colony of five hundred survived. Archer and Ratcliffe were among those who died. In the spring the colony was abandoned by Gates, who finally had arrived; but before the colonists could leave Chesapeake Bay, the arrival of a new governor, Lord de la Warre, stopped the exodus.

In the meanwhile, the Virginia Company had sought to counteract the rumors current in London concerning the colonists' misadventures. The company published a *True and sincere declaration of the purposes and ends of the Plantation begun in Virginia* (London, 1610); but this publication was not based on any real understanding of what had happened. When even worse reports reached London, the company published, later the same year, a revised version of the *True declaration,* "*with a confutation of such scandalous reports as have tended to the disgrace of so worthy an enterprise.*" This work was an effort to defend the colony's failures with excuses, some of them untrue. Smith knew the true story from his experiences, from what returning colonists had reported, and from the accounts sent back from Virginia. He and some of the other returned colonists were eager for the truth to be known. With some difficulty they got their story published, after a clergyman named William Symonds had edited it into shape. Perhaps because the London booksellers did not want to offend the Virginia Company, whose accounts were to be corrected by Symonds's book, *A Map of Virginia* was published at Oxford, in 1612.

IX "A Description of Virginia"

A Map of Virginia is in two parts. Smith contributed the first part, thirty-nine pages of "A Description of the Country, the Commodities, People, Government, and Religion, Written by Captaine Smith, sometimes Governour of the Countrey." (The running title is "The voyages and discoveries of Captaine John Smith in Virginia.") Though his name is not listed as an author, Smith also had a hand in the second part, which provides a valuable account of "the proceedings and accidents" of the colonists from 1607 to 1612. Smith republished this account with a good many additions and changes as the third book of the *Generall Historie.*

In addition to these two parts which constitute 149 quarto pages, the book includes a map of Virginia, engraved by William Hole according to Smith's directions. The copper plate prepared by Hole was used again and again—in all, ten times, with additions being made each time, through the year 1632. The map was published separately, and it also accompanied the *Generall Historie.* It includes pictorial inserts, most of them based on De Bry's engravings of John White's drawings, which were prepared to accompany the 1590 edition of Thomas Hariot's *Brief and True Relation*. One pictures Powhatan as he appeared to Smith when he was captured in 1607. The map, a very accurate one, is especially valuable since it is, according to Ben McCary, "practically the only record of the location of the Indian tribes of Virginia in the early seventeenth century."[12]

This map and Smith's description are both enlargements of an earlier map and a description ("a relation of the countries and nations that inhabit" Virginia) sent by Smith from Virginia in 1608; but neither is extant in its original form. The published map and description are among the most valuable of Smith's legacies, though not primarily as literature. This is not to say that the "Description" is not well written. As Howard Mumford Jones says, " ... in both style and organization it shows how excellent an observer Smith could be, how trenchantly he wrote. ... "[13]

The "Description" is perhaps Smith's most permanently interesting work. His biographers have told the story of his life well; the story of the early days of the Virginia colony are more fully told in modern histories (though, of course, they lack Smith's sense of immediacy); Smith's works on New England seem somewhat dated because of their propaganda approach, which many readers find unattractive. But the "Description" is so consistently entertaining that it is surprising that it has never been republished as a separate work.

Smith's career and training were ideal preparations for the composition of this book. He was very different from those he disparages in the concluding pages, who were "for the most part of ... tender educations and small experience in martial accidents" (83). He knew other lands and other cultures; he could keep his wits in the midst of great danger; he had seen more of Virginia than any other man; and he had known the Indians as a trader, fighter, and captive.

Before *A Map* was published, Smith gave his friend Samuel Purchas a manuscript description of Virginia to use in the preparation of the first edition of *Purchas his Pilgrimage*. Though this work did not appear until 1613, the year following the publication of *A Map*, Purchas's big book seems to have been in press earlier. Probably Purchas used what Smith gave William Symonds to edit into publishable form. He called it on page 635 "Cap. Smith, M. S." (In the 1625 *Pilgrimes*, Purchas clearly used the published book, not the manuscript or the *Pilgrimage* version; he reprinted the whole of the "Description.") The *Pilgrimage* version may provide a good idea of what Smith wrote for Symonds, though it may have been revised somewhat by Purchas himself. These parallel passages are from the two printed versions:

Purchas, *Pilgrimage*
The chief god they worship is the devil, which they call *Oke.*

They have conference with him, and fashion themselves unto his shape. In their temples they have his image ill-favoredly made, painted, adorned with chains, copper, and beads, and covered with a skin.

By him is commonly the sepulcher of their kings, whose bodies are first boweled, then dried on a hurdle,

and have about the joints chains of copper, beads, and other like trash;

then lapped in white skins, and rolled in mats, and entombed in arches made of mats, the remnant

of their wealth being set at their feet. These temples

and bodies are kept by their priests. (p. 639)

Smith, *A Map*
But their chief god they worship is the devil. Him they call *Oke* and serve him more of feare than love. They say they have conference with him, and fashion themselves as near to his shape as they can imagine. In their temples they have his image evil-favoredly carved and then painted and adorned with chains, copper, and beads, and covered with a skin, in such manner as the deformity may well suit with such a god. By him is commonly the sepulcher of their kings. Their bodies are first boweled, then dried upon hurdles till they be very dry, and so about the most of their joints and neck they hang bracelets or chains of copper, pearl, and such like, as they use to wear; their inwards they stuff with copper beads and cover with a skin, hatchets, and such trash. Then lap they them very carefully in white skins, and so roll them in mats for their winding sheets. And in the tomb, which is an arch made of mats, they lay them orderly. What remaineth of this kind of wealth their kings have, they set at their feet in baskets. These temples and bodies are kept by their priests. (p. 75)

The version in *A Map* is full of editorializing such as one might expect of a Christian clergyman. The *Pilgrimage* version is more condensed. Purchas's version is probably closer to what Smith wrote, though Purchas may have trimmed what Smith gave him, as he seems also to have done with Smith's autobiography. (See Chapter 7.)

Smith began the work with a vocabulary of Indian words and phrases. Besides the Indian words for numbers and other common expressions, Smith demonstrated the Algonkian language with such revealing phrases as "Bid Pocahontas bring hither two little baskets and I will give her white beads to make her a chain," and "Run you to the king Mawmarynough and bid him come hither" (46).

X Smith as Natural Historian

The "Description" proper begins with geography: the climate, the shape of their land, the rivers, a catalogue of the inhabitants. This section is full of interesting observations, some of which reveal an eye sensitive to beauty: "The country is not mountainous nor yet low but such pleasant plain hills and fertile valleys, one prettily crossing another, and watered so ·conveniently with their sweet brooks and crystal springs as if art itself had devised them" (49). Smith was especially impressed with the Susquehannock Indians, who lived at the northern end of Chesapeake Bay.

Such great and well proportioned men [noted Smith] are seldom seen, for they seemed like giants to the English, yea and to the neighbors, yet seemed of an honest and simple disposition [and were] with much ado restrained from adoring the discoverers as gods. Those are the most strange people of all those countries, both in language and attire. For their language it may well beseem their proportions, sounding from them as it were a great voice in a vault or cave, as an echo. Their attire is the skins of bears and wolves. Some have cassocks made of bears' heads and skins that a man's neck goes through the skin's neck, and the ears of the bear fastened to his shoulders behind, the nose and teeth hanging down his breast, and at the end of the nose hung a bear's paw. (54)

The next sections of the "Description," which resemble Hariot's *Brief and True Report,* deal with the useful plants growing naturally and in cultivated fashion, and the products which Virginia could produce for export. This last section is Smith's extended propaganda plea for America, the sort of thing which became his chief concern when he found that he was not able to return to either Virginia or New England. He argued that Virginia could produce the same commodities which bring most wealth to England's competitors: Muscovy, Poland, Sweden, France, Spain, Italy, and Holland. Virginian products were within a hundred miles "to be had, either ready provided by nature or else to be prepared, were there but industrious men to labor" (64).

Despite the unrestrained optimism of this passage and a few others, the tone of most of the work is cautious; Smith's motive was "to satisfy my friends of the true worth and quality of Virginia" (82). He had little use for those who wanted quick and easy wealth, particularly that obtained from gold. He reported little certain information on mineral resources since skilled refiners had not been available. He scoffed at those who found "shining stones and spangles" and flattered themselves "in their own vain conceits to have been supposed that they were not" (61).

But, more than his optimism or his practicality, what impresses one most about Smith's account is his extensive knowledge. Sometimes it is revealed in minor observations, as when he noted that Indian peas resemble what the Italians call *fagioli* and that Indian beans resemble what the Turks call *garnases*. But chiefly one is impressed by Smith's knowledge of natural phenomena: Indian medicines and herbs, seventeen varieties of animals (including bears "very little in comparison of those of Muscovia and Tartaria"), and twenty kinds of fish.

XI Smith on the Virginia Indians

Smith devoted the second half of his "Description" to the Indians: their appearance, way of life, hunting and fishing, warfare, medicine, religion, and government. As Jones has observed, Smith did not always comprehend what he saw, "but his devouring eye has missed nothing."[14] Since he made his observations, as he himself noted, mainly as a prisoner of the Indians (70), the acuteness of his report is all the more remarkable.

Two articles have been devoted to Smith's view of the Indians. The earlier (and more superficial) study argues that Smith was "a candid, liberal, and fair reporter of the Indians."[15] The later article is an effort to see Smith's attitude in its historical context. Its author, Miss Keith Glenn, observed that some Englishmen considered it unlawful to colonize lands occupied by other peoples, especially since cruelty and oppressive treatment of the natives were a likely result, as Spanish practices had shown. Therefore much was made of the missionary value of colonization as a justification. This view implied a kind of equality between white men and Indians. Furthermore, the Virginia Company had specifically instructed the colonists: " ... you must have great care not to offend the naturals, if you can eschew it."[16]

But, in Miss Glenn's view, Smith considered that the London instructions were intended to be a means to an end—the establishment of a successful colony—and that the Indians were in fact obstacles to the achievement of this objective. Therefore, he adopted a very different attitude from the official one. He believed that the Indians should be subjugated and, once put in their place, made to work for the colonists in such tasks as they could best perform: growing corn, hunting, and fishing. This policy was offensive to the London Virginia Company until Indian massacres of the English made it seem wiser.[17] Miss Glenn's interpretation is sound and helpful, though it overlooks one fact: Smith considered the Indians useful as guides on how to survive in the American wilderness. In the "Description" he sought, in part, to be a reporter on the Indians because to know their ways would permit one to learn from them.

Roy Harvey Pearce has noted that Smith assumed "the naturally minimal order of savage life, with its natural aspiration towards the higher life of Christian civility."[18] This assumption was, of course, common to Englishmen of Smith's time. It is, however, hardly fair to write, as did Pearce, that Smith saw the Indians as mere savages. He did indeed write that "some are of disposition fearfull, some bold, most cautelous, all *savage*" (65). But clearly he was more impressed with their abilities, as craftsmen, as woodsmen, and as warriors. (Smith was always the soldier.) "They are very strong, of an able body and full of agility, able to endure to lie in the woods by the fire in the worst of winter, or in the weeds and grass, in *ambuscado* in the summer" (65). He looked at their skill in warfare like an old soldier: in the attack there is "on each flank a sergeant, and in the rear an officer for lieutenant, all duly keeping their orders, yet leaping and singing after their accustomed tune, which they use only in wars" (72).

Though it was with some disgust that Smith noted the "the common sort have scarce to cover their nakedness but with grass, the leaves of trees, and such like," he described with satisfaction a mantle of feathers " so prettily wrought and woven with threads that nothing could be discerned but the feathers" (66). Smith was not interested in emphasizing the inferiority of the Indians; on the contrary, many of his comparisons stress their abilities. Thus he noted that they do not use oars but instead "use paddles and sticks, with which they will row faster than our barges" (69). But it was the Indians' adaptability that Smith especially admired: they "know all the advantages and places most frequented with deer, beasts, fish, fowl, roots, and berries" (69).

Smith was an optimistic, practical, careful observer, working indeed from the assumptions of his time but showing real interest in and rarely condescension towards the Indians. He was surprisingly objective, if tough-minded. Thus Smith reported without comment that in the holes in their ears some Indians wear "a small green- and yellow-colored snake, near half a yard in length, which, crawling and lapping herself about his neck, oftentimes familiarly would kiss his lips" (66). Indians treat a guest generously, Smith reported, again without comment: "at night, where his lodging is appointed, they set a woman fresh painted red with *pocones* and oil, to be his bedfellow" (73). Whether Smith received this generous treatment is not reported.

In his comments on Indian religion Smith is perhaps least perceptive, but his account is interesting, comprehensive, full of detail. His reactions to Indian religion occasionally reflect his values (he had definite religious convictions), as when he noted that "before their dinners and suppers, the better sort will take the first bit and cast it into the fire, which is all the grace they are known to use" (77).

Perry Miller has demonstrated that, according to the early literature of Virginia, a prime motive in the establishment of the colony was the conversion of the Indians to Christianity.[19] Smith had little to say about this goal. He did indeed characterize Virginia as "a nurse for soldiers, a practice for mariners, a trade for merchants, a reward for the good, and that which is most of all, a business (most acceptable to God) to bring such poor infidels to the true knowledge of God and His Holy Gospel" (64). But Smith's observations on the Indians do not suggest that his statement is to be taken with much seriousness. Though he was appalled by the Indians' worship of the ugly, evil idol *Oke*, and though he lamented their ignorance of their creator, he was only too much aware that the best endeavors of the English "to divest them from their blind idolatry" got them nowhere. (The Indians merely considered that their gods were inferior to the stronger ones of the English.)

The most unsatisfactory aspect of Smith's treatment of the Indians is his report of an annual "sacrifice of children." Smith described as much as he (or another Englishman) saw; but important parts of the ceremony, he noted, were "not seen" (78). Ben McCary identified the ceremony with the *Huskanaw*, which was a kind of initiation or hardening and testing.[20]

In the last section on Indian government, Smith again emphasized the capacities of the Indians, not their inferiority: "their magistrates for good commanding and their people for due subjection and obeying excell many places that would be counted very civil" (79). Most of the chapter is devoted to Powhatan, the Indian emperor—his jurisdiction, dealings with the inferior kings or werowances, treasury, justice, system of punishments. Among the punishments is one with which Smith nearly had personal experience, according to the account in the *Generall Historie:* "Sometimes he causeth the heads of them that offend him to be laid upon the altar or sacrificing stone, and one with clubs beats out their brains" (81). If Smith barely escaped this form of execution, it is not surprising that he next cited the excruciating means used to kill George Cusson, who had been a member of Smith's party when he was captured: "he causeth him to be tied to a tree, and with mussel shells or reeds, the executioner cutteth off his joints one after another, ever casting what they cut off into the fire. Then doth he proceed with shells and reeds to case the skin from his head and face. Then do they rip his belly and so burn him with the tree and all" (81–82).

XII Setting the Record Straight

The last pages of the "Description" demonstrate once again that *A Map of Virginia* was written to set the record straight. Here Smith attacked in blunt fashion those colonists who pretended to be experts on things Virginian though they "were scarce ever ten miles from Jamestown" (82). These same, he protested, were themselves a "plague to us in Virginia." Nevertheless, all went well "so long after as I did govern there, until I left the country" (84).

With this personal note, Smith ended the work. A proud man, Smith chose not to write an extended defense of himself, though he expressed satisfaction that the second part of the *Map* provided a full report. Indeed, it is a vindication of Smith; and, lest he should appear thin-skinned, it should be noted that the authors of the second part report "foul slanders" of Smith "urged for truths by many a hundred that do still not spare to spread them, say them, and swear them" (169). But, instead of writing a personal testament, Smith wrote a precise account of the Virginia he knew so well; packed with information, objective yet far from cold, detailed but not dull, his is the work of an immensely perceptive man whose bold adventures led him to know what a less active man never could have discovered.

The "Description" is highly valued by ethnologists and anthropologists.[21] With the broader view of history which has been adopted in the twentieth century Smith's brief study should be recognized as of great historical importance. Because Smith's later original contributions to the *Generall Historie* in Book III are fragmentary and less objective, the "Description" is really Smith's most important contribution to historical studies. A *True Relation* is also important since, unlike the discussion of his Virginia years in the *Historie*, it is all his own.

CHAPTER 4

The Compiler: *The Generall Historie*

C APTAIN JOHN SMITH'S most famous work is the *Generall Historie of Virginia, New England, and the Summer Isles.* It has been judged worthy to rank with the histories of William Bradford, Edward Johnson, and John Winthrop;[1] indeed, Smith has been called "the father of Anglo-American History."[2] The *Generall Historie* is complex, uneven, and controversial. According to one commentator, "John Smith's *Generall Historie* is an important part of the deeper cultural consciousness" which has sustained the "perennial faith in the promise of American life." The heart of the *Historie,* Books III and IV, "have a dramatic rhythm and an exciting vividness that charmed Americans for generations."[3] For another reader, "Smith's so-called History of Virginia is not a history at all; but chiefly an eulogy of Smith and a lampoon of his peers."[4] The *Generall Historie* is an important but much misunderstood book; and a particular need is a study of Smith's role as compiler.

I Circumstances of Composition

The origin of the *Historie* appears to have been an occasion in April, 1621, when John Smythe of Nibley, a Gloucestershire man who had invested in the Virginia Company of London, moved at a meeting of the company that the Virginia colony would benefit from the publication of "a fair and perspicious history, compiled of that country, from her discovery to this day."[5] Such a "general history," as he called it, would serve as a memorial of the colony and preserve for posterity truth which might otherwise suffer the ravages of time—or so thought John Smythe.

His motion was commended by those attending the meeting, but no action was taken. At the time, the colony was in good health; it seemed at last to be thriving. But in March, 1622, the Indians of Virginia rose and killed about four hundred colonists. Captain John Smith soon requested the Virginia Company to send him, with one hundred soldiers and thirty sailors, "to enforce the savages to leave their country, or bring them in that fear and subjection that every man should follow their business securely." (Smith published his letter in the *Historie,* pages 588–90.) The

Company expressed little intelligent interest in Smith's plan, however, and Smith was again frustrated.[6] In his disappointment, he sought to assist the cause of American colonization by writing a history. As Bradford Smith put it, "Writing was not his life but a substitute for living."[7]

John Smith was a likely man to pick up a proposal for a history of Virginia, for he knew the colony well, cared much for its welfare, and was experienced as a writer. Since he also knew New England, he decided to include it in his history; moreover, he could thereby use his earlier writings on New England. A more skillful writer, William Strachey, had begun *The Historie of Travell into Virginia Britania* (which for him also included New England); but he had given up the work before his death.[8] How Smith chose to include Bermuda is not clear; perhaps he came across sources and decided to use them.

By September, 1622, Smith had already prepared much of Book I of the *Historie*,[9] and the following year he published a prospectus so detailed as to indicate that the work was well along, and perhaps completed.[10] This prospectus was intended to raise funds to support publication; he pleaded he needed nearly a hundred pounds. How much was raised in this fashion, if any, is not known; but Smith did find a patron in the very wealthy Duchess of Richmond and Lenox, to whom the *Historie* is dedicated, and without whose bounty, Smith wrote, "it had died in the womb" (277).

The completed book was published in 1624, a handsome folio volume of 241 pages, with an attractive engraved title page; four engraved maps (Ould Virginia, or the Roanoke colony area, Virginia, the Summer Isles, and New England); and, in some copies, portraits of Pocahontas and the Duchess of Richmond and Lenox. Both an ordinary and a large paper edition were published. Two printers prepared the work, and by a miscalculation there are no pages numbered 95–104, though there is no gap in the work itself. Six later editions or issues of the *Historie* were published between 1626 and 1632, but these prove to have been unsold copies of the original printing, with new title pages and some changes in the map. The *Historie* is decorated with a flowery dedication and a good deal of verse: sixteen complimentary poems, including ones by Samuel Purchas and John Donne. Also throughout the text bits of more or less appropriate verse appear, largely translations of Classical authors, borrowed with a few changes from Bishop Martin Fotherby's *Atheomastix* (1622). Smith seems to have picked up the idea of using poetry in this fashion from George Sandys' *Relation of a Journey*, published in 1615.[11]

Smith set out to make the *Historie,* it is important to note, a collection such as those made by Richard Hakluyt and Samuel Purchas, especially Purchas, whom he knew and who assisted him. Smith made this point clear by appending to the table of contents a couplet.

> It's not his part that is the best translator
> To render word for word to every author.

Like Purchas, Smith served not so much as historian as compiler, though not a *mere* compiler, he insisted. "I am no compiler by hearsay," he wrote in the dedicatory epistle, "but have been a real actor. I take myself to have a property in them, and therefore have been bold to challenge them to come under the reach of my rough pen" (275). Smith's most substantial contribution appears in Book III, in which there is almost ten thousand words of new material. (See Chapter 6).

The first four books of the *Historie* deal mainly with Virginia. Book I provides a history of the Roanoke colony and early visits to New England; Book II describes the land and people of the Jamestown area; and Books III and IV relate the story of the Virginia colony through 1624. Book V deals with the Bermudas, and Book VI reports the history of New England beginning with Smith's visit in 1614. In the *True Travels* (1630), Smith continued and extended the *Historie,* with brief reports on English colonial efforts in Guiana and the West Indies.

The *Historie* begins with a brief preface "of four points." Three cite the virtues of having colonies: they bring honor to the King by spreading Christianity and enriching the English monarchy; they serve as an excellent investment; and they provide an opportunity for the industrious and virtuous to get ahead. The last point indicates Smith's good intentions: " ... now my care hath been that my relations should give every man their concern, their due. But had I not discovered and lived in the most of those parts, I could not possibly have collected the substantial truth from such a number of variable relations, that would make a volume of at least a thousand sheets [A thousand sheets would be four thousand folio pages.]" (279).

II Book One

Without further explanation—and some additions would have been helpful—the work begins. Seven paragraphs tell in extremely condensed form the mythological and historical discovery

of America, English explorations under the Cabots, and the work
of Frobisher and Gilbert. The first block of material follows: a
report on the first voyage of 1584 made to America under Sir
Walter Raleigh. Smith's source is an account in Richard Hakluyt's
Principal Voyages written by one of the two captains of the vessels making the voyage.[12] At first Smith shifted from the first
person of his source to the third person, but in the second paragraph he picked up the point of view of his source. Smith summarized and at times rearranged the order of his source, an
indication that he took some time to prepare his work. At one
point he noted that he was using "the author's own phrase" (306);
in fact, nearly everything is in the phrasing of Smith's author. At
another point Smith used the expression "the author sayth," perhaps because he was doubtful that the statement supplied was
correct. In about half as many words as his original, Smith told the
interesting and important story of the voyage.

Smith turned back to the *Principal Voyages* for his next account,
which in Hakluyt's collection immediately follows the one that
Smith had just used. This time the source is a log of another
voyage to Roanoke and "an account of the particularities of the
employment of the Englishmen left in Virginia."[13] Smith, who
made no additions, condensed thirteen pages to four. Then he
used another document from Hakluyt, an account by the governor
of the colony, Ralph Lane.

Although Smith's next source, Thomas Hariot's *Brief and True
Relation*, was reprinted—in condensed form—in Hakluyt, Smith
seems to have turned to the original account. He reprinted only a
little material from Hariot, however, presumably because in Book
II Smith's own "Description of Virginia" covers much the same
material. Thus he noted that the North Carolina Indians' "cloth-
ing, towns, houses, wars, arts, tools, handicrafts, and educations
are much like them in that part of Virginia we now inhabit; which
at large you may read in the description thereof. But the relation
of their religion is strange, as this author reporteth" (320–21).
Then follows an account of the Indians' religion.

Smith continued to follow Hakluyt all the way to the end of the
account on Roanoke, except perhaps for the Hariot *Report*. Then
with only a part of an original sentence for transition, he began to
borrow again. "All hopes of Virginia thus abandoned, it lay dead
and obscured from 1590 till this year 1602, that Captain Gosnold,
with thirty-two and himself in a small bark, set sail from Dartmouth upon the twenty-sixth of March" (332). Smith's borrowing
is from John Brereton's *Brief and True Relation* (London, 1602),

which tells of a voyage to Cape Cod. Smith revised distances and dates, condensed Brereton's effective descriptions, and weakened an interesting report; this part is, therefore, much less attractive than it might have been.

Though most readers of Book I are aware that little of Smith's material is original, just how closely Smith followed his sources is not so evident. Here is how he revised a portion of Brereton's account:

Brereton	*Smith*
But not to cloy you with	... but not to cloy you with
particular rehearsal of	particulars,
such things as God and	what God
Nature hath bestowed on	and nature hath bestowed on
these places, in comparison	those places, I refer you to
whereof, the most fertile part	the author's own writing
of all England is (of itself)	at large. (334)
but barren. (7)	

Smith was enthusiastic about New England, but he was determined to be cautious in his commendations.

For the remaining two portions of Book I, on voyages to New England, Smith used two reports which Samuel Purchas was to publish in 1625. The former of these may have been included in the materials collected by Hakluyt and obtained by Purchas after Hakluyt's death; it is entitled by Purchas "A Voyage set out from the Citie of Bristoll."[14] The second is James Rosier's *True Relation* (1605), for which Smith seems to have used the abridged version —he may have used printer's proofs—that was to appear in *Purchas His Pilgrimes*.[15]

Book I of Smith's *Historie* is a comprehensive account of Pre-Jamestown English exploration in America. It was easily compiled, for Smith had only to consult Hakluyt's great *Voyages*, his friend Purchas's collection of documents, and probably two additional published accounts, Hariot's and Brereton's. Everything in Book I is available elsewhere, in fuller form. A convenient prologue is perhaps the best way to characterize Book I.

III Book Two

Entitled "The Sixth Voyage. 1606. To another part of Virginia," Book II is a reprint of Smith's own "Description of Virginia." Smith made no attempt to justify its inclusion: it is simply another document relating to Virginia, and he made very few revisions. He shifted the narrative portions from the third to the first person, presumably to make the book correspond to other narratives; and he made a very few deletions and additions. He noted, for example, that an Indian ceremony which he had described in the original work was more properly characterized later as part of the narrative of his captivity in Book III. To his expression of regret that the Indians were ignorant of true religion, he added in the *Historie*, "and we had not language sufficient so plainly to express it as make them understand it, which God grant they may" (374).

Smith sought to impose on his materials no unity of any kind. He aimed merely to eliminate from the sources he had collected whatever "would tire any wise man" (784): patents, treaties, directions, and the like. Some portions of the *Historie* do hang together through a vague sense of Smith's personality that shows through the writing, but very little of this quality is found in Book I, where Smith's task was simply that of digester of other men's writings, or even in Book II, where, although the whole is Smith's writing, the tone is the least personal of his original works.

IV Book Three

Book III, in which nearly a fourth is Smith's writing especially for the *Historie*, is quite different. Since Smith's reputation as a historian rests mostly on this book, it is best discussed in Chapter 6. It suffices to say here that it is a coherent account of the events that took place in Virginia from 1607 to 1609, based on the report prepared by Smith's friends and published in 1612, as part of *A Map of Virginia*. Smith was fortunate to have such a substantial and lively basis for the book.

V Book Four

Book IV is of almost equal importance to the student of Smith's writings and very important for a consideration of his work as a compiler. It tells the story of Virginia after Smith's departure. From what his supporters had written about the conduct of the colony by those who succeeded him in its government (in "The Proceedings," Smith's basis for Book III), it might be expected that Smith would indulge in some special pleading,[16] but one is scarcely prepared for what is found. Even an admirer of Smith would find it difficult to praise this collection of miscellaneous documents.

After a clear and coherent beginning, Smith included in almost random fashion whatever he could locate related to the colony in any way: an announcement of a lottery for Virginia, an extended account of a sea fight in the West Indies (one of the participating ships was on its way to Virginia), a list of items that each immigrant to Virginia should possess, and a long list (twelve pages) of the "adventurers for Virginia" "according to a printed book." One theme runs through Book IV: Smith was the only real expert on Virginia, and he alone knew what should have been done and what should be done now.

Editorializing of various kinds occupies nearly a fourth of the book. Smith described his project for subduing the Indians who had recently massacred the settlers; he printed "a brief relation written by Captain Smith to his Majesty's Commissioners for the reform of Virginia, concerning some aspersions against it"; and seven answers that Smith had supplied the commissioners. One of Smith's motives in preparing the *Historie* may have been his desire to hasten the collapse of the Virginia Company, but it was officially dissolved just before the *Historie* appeared.

At the end of the book Smith attempted to justify his procedure of including all manner of information. Perhaps he recognized the weakness of this portion, but his apology is inadequate since it does not explain why the book is so devoted to Smith's case for himself:

Thus far I have travelled in this wilderness of Virginia, not being ignorant [that] for all my pains this discourse will be wrested, tossed, and turned as many ways as there is leaves; that I have writ too much of some, too little of others, and many such like objections. To such I must answer, in the Company's name I was requested to do it. If any have concealed their approved experiences from my knowledge, they must excuse me. As for every fatherless or stolen relation, I leave them to the charge of them that desire them. (622)

What Smith wrote may be true, though there is no evidence that he was requested by the Virginia Company to prepare the *Historie;* and he made no effort to defend the company but instead was often critical of it. It should be said for Smith that a bibliography of contemporary accounts of Virginia indicates little of significance that Smith might but did not use.[17] A notable exception, perhaps, is an unpublished account by John Rolfe on the state of the colony in 1616, a period rather neglected in the *Historie;* but Smith may not have known about this narrative. Later historians have of course been able to draw on many sources that Smith did not have access to.

Smith reprinted in abridged form a good many pages of writings previously published, among the best covered period being the years reported by two of these documents: Ralph Hamor's *True Discourse of the Present Estate of Virginia* (1615), which deals with the years 1611–14, and Edward Waterhouse's *A Declaration of the state of the colony and affairs in Virginia* (1622), which reports on the massacre of 1622. Smith condensed, rephrased, and revised these works; and he even on occasion argued with his source. Thus Hamor's criticism of one Jeffrey Abbots aroused Smith to comment: "Here I entreat your patience for an apology, though not a pardon. This Jeffrey Abbots, however this author censures him, and the Governor executes him, I know he had long served both in Ireland and Netherlands. Here he was a sergeant of my company, and I never saw in Virginia a more sufficient soldier, less turbulent, a better wit, more hardy or industrious, nor any more forward to cut off them that sought to abandon the country or wrong the colony"(508).

Hamor's account is very detailed, and Smith's digest is an intelligent one. He trimmed Hamor's propaganda, but on occasion inserted some of his own:

Hamor	*Smith*
Pocahontas (whose fame hath even been spread in England by the title of non parella of Virginia). . . . (4)	Pocahontas, whom Captain Smith's relations entitleth the numparell of Virginia . . . .(511)

Book IV does include some private letters not available elsewhere, for example a few pages on Lord de la Warre as governor by William Box (501–504). But this section is indeed fundamentally Captain John Smith's apologia. He listed for the King's commissioners the great accomplishments of the years when he was present in Virginia: the subjection of the Indians, the shipment of valuable commodities to England (timber, pitch, tar, samples of ore, and the like); the building of Jamestown with forty or fifty houses and three forts; and the planting of corn:

We had but six ships to transport and supply us, and but 277 men, boys, and women, by whose labors Virginia being brought to this kind of perfection, the most difficulties past, and the foundation thus laid by this small means. Yet because we had done no more, they called in our commission, took a new in their own names, and appointed us near as many offices and officers as I had soldiers, that neither knew us nor we them—without our consents or knowledge. Since, there have gone more than one hundred ships of other proportions, and eight or ten thousand people. Now if you please to compare what hath been spent, sent, discovered, and done this fifteen years by that we did in the three first years, and every governor that hath been there since give you but such an account as this, you may easily see what hath been the cause of those disasters in Virginia. (612–13)

Smith's explanation of Virginia's problems was, clearly, the absence of one Captain Smith from Virginia. He surely could not have supposed that he was aiding the Virginia Company with this kind of comment.

Elsewhere Book IV contains a long digression in which Smith protested that the "first adventurers" had not benefited from the colony as was intended and that many of the most deserving and industrious (including, by implication, himself) had profited far less than the nobility and gentry (526–27). Perhaps the subjective, opinionated tone of these comments is best explained by Smith's statement that he may be "too bold to censure other men's actions" when he himself had not been in Virginia for years, but that others who had never been to Virginia had censured him. Lest his readers suppose that he was merely being vindictive, he declared that his motives were "the glory of God, the honor of my country, and the public good" (585).

Much of the history which Book IV surveys demonstrated to Smith the wisdom of his own policies. He pointed to the lack of continuity in leadership and to the weakness of the governors, especially in dealing with the Indians. The massacre of 1622 was for Smith a complete vindication of his own tough Indian policy, and he repeated his recommendations for dealing with the Indians so frequently that he could write at one point: "The manner how to surpress them is so often related and approved, I omit it here. And you have twenty examples of the Spaniards how they got the West Indies and forced the treacherous and rebellious infidels to do all manner of drudgery work and slavery for them, themselves living like soldiers upon the fruits of their labors. This will make us more circumspect and be an example to posterity. (But, I say, this might as well have been put in practice sixteen years ago as now)" (579). This passage is followed by three pages of "Encouragements": obstacles should lead only to greater efforts, according to Smith, who again cited Spanish experience.

Smith's optimism frequently saved his editorializing from tediousness. Similarly appealing is his sense of America's limitless possibilities: "Let us with all speed take the priority of place, in choosing the best seats of the county, which now by vanquishing the savages, is like to offer a more fair and ample choice of fruitful habitations than hitherto our gentleness and fair comportments could attain unto" (582).

But objectionable the editorializing still is because the accounts which constitute Book IV are primarily narratives of adventures, full of encounters with the Indians, and the regular interjection of "Captain Smith's opinion" is an annoying interruption. Furthermore, Smith was probably ignorant of the work of the London Virginia Company, the routine of whose meetings would have seemed both dull and unimportant to Smith. J. Franklin Jameson's observation is relevant: Smith "writes, by preference, of encounters, of explorations, of opportunities for present gains, as one who is directing a band of adventurers. . . . "[18] As a result of the emphasis on action (and the editorializing), Smith's history lacks perspective and balance: it contains close-ups but no background is visible, no panoramic views. In Book IV even Smith's ability to compose an orderly series of pictures collapsed. His frustrations and disappointments got the best of him, and his carefully edited collection of documents degenerated into a vindication of John Smith.

A final example of how Smith's egotism damaged the plan of the *Historie* should suffice. In Book IV Smith included his earliest account of his rescue by Pocahontas—the earliest if the letter which he published is indeed "an abstract" of "a little book" written to Queen Anne to make Pocahontas's virtues known to the Queen and her court. Smith's excuse for publishing it is merely that it relates to a Virginian Indian's visit to London in 1616. According to this account, "After some six weeks' fatting amongst those savage courtiers, at the minute of my execution she hazarded the beating out of her own brains to save mine, and not only that but so prevailed with her father that I was safely conducted to Jamestown ... " (531). Alexander Brown, usually unfair to Smith, was perhaps not far wrong in his comment: "The letter was superfluous so far as the interests of Pocahontas were concerned, and the writer seems to be well aware of this fact, for although it is written in her interest, it does not lose sight of the interests of Smith for a moment."[19] The Pocahontas letter occupies several pages of Book IV.

VI Book Five

Book V is different from the other parts of the *Historie* because Smith never visited the Bermudas, the subject of the book; therefore, he found little occasion for editorializing. The book is mostly a digest of one source, Nathaniel Butler's *The Historye of the Burmudaes,* a work available to Smith in manuscript.[20] For the early pages, which describe the islands and their plants and animals, Smith also used another manuscript account, Richard Norwood's *Insularum de la Bermuda Detectio.*[20] A few pages concerning the shipwreck of Somers, Gates, and Newport in 1609 are based on Sylvester Jourdain's *Plaine Description of the Barmudas* (London, 1613). Smith wrote of having borrowed also from "divers others," some of whom he names; but—except for some of the descriptions of the natural life of the islands, the story of Henry May's shipwreck, and the last few pages on recent events (probably based on oral accounts)—Smith seems to have used only the sources noted. He made the book into a coherent, continuous narrative.

Butler's history is a book-length work which Smith trimmed severely; occasionally he supplemented it and brought it up to date. Thus he noted the names of six governors who succeeded Richard More (648), and he discussed the term of office of each, as Butler had not. A specimen of Smith's use of Butler indicates the kind of trimming to be found in the *Historie.*

Butler	Smith
... he absolutely resolved with all expedition to frame and erect a very substantial and brave cedar house. (109)	... they built a fair house of cedar. ... (665)

Perhaps the most significant and revealing adaptation that Smith makes is his neglect of Butler's long account of the power struggles in England, an indication of Smith's preference for action over problems of administration. The account of the case drawn up against Butler by Sir Edwin Sandys (642–65), which sheds light on the political context of English colonization, is all but omitted in the *Historie,* where Smith merely wrote: "and withall, a strange and wonderful report of much complaint made against the Governor to the Company in England, by some of them returned in the last year's shipping" (678).

On the other hand, the very practical Smith amplified Butler's brief comment on the colonists sent to Bermuda: " ... so ill chosen they were (for they had been taken out of Newgate), that small hope of good was to be had of them ... " (204). Smith put it more strongly: the colonists were "of such bad condition that it seemed they had picked the males out of Newgate, the females from Bridewell. As the governor found it his best course to grant out the women to such as were so greedy of wives and would needs have them for better or worse, and the men he placed in the King's castle for soldiers" (676).

Smith's history of Bermuda is a workmanlike job, except for a few spots where haste seems to have caused him to misrepresent his source. The book lacks both the strengths and the weaknesses of Book IV; it covers the subject better but without the sense of being authoritative. Since it is based on sources which were not available in published form until more than two hundred and fifty years had passed, Smith made an important contribution to knowledge in this book.

VII Book Six

Like Book II, Book VI is based on Smith's earlier work. Entitled "The Generall Historie of New England," it lacks effective organization because Smith's two earlier writings on New England do not fit neatly into a historical framework. Smith drew a good many pages of material from *A Description of New England* (1616), a mixture of description, adventure, narrative, and propaganda. This work was revised more thoroughly than "The Description of Virginia" had been for Book II, mostly to bring it up to date. The revision noted below must have been painful to make!

1616 version	*1624 version*
From thence doth stretch into the sea the fair headland Tragabigzanda, fronted with three isles called the three Turks' heads . . . . (204)	From hence doth stretch into the sea the fair headland Tragabigzanda, now called Cape Ann, fronted with three isles we called the three Turks' heads . . . . (718)

Tragabigzanda and the Turks' heads recalled Smith's experiences as warrior and slave in the Balkans and Turkey in his pre-Virginia years. Prince Charles had renamed at Smith's request many New England places listed on Smith's map, one for Charles's mother Anne.

Some parts of the earlier version were rewritten—to improve them, apparently. Thus Smith clarified and made more vivid the very obscure account in *A Description of New England* of how he had attempted to go to America in 1615 and had found himself, because of a mutiny, on board a French vessel; he was abandoned "in his cap, breeches, and waistcoat, alone among the Frenchmen; his clothes, arms, and what he had, our mutineers shared among them . . . "(735).

Smith next picked up from the revised and enlarged edition of *New England Trials* (1622). Since this work was written shortly before the *Historie,* it was but slightly revised, mostly by the addition of a few paragraphs. Into the midst of the work he inserted (749–60) a portion of "Mourt's" *Relation* (1622), an account of the Pilgrims now thought to be the work of Edward Winslow and William Bradford.[22] Smith chose to revise his source at times, once in a quite effective fashion:

"Mourt"	*Smith*
... we much fearing that if we should stay any longer, we should not be able to recover home for want of strength. (67)	... our heads were as light for want of sleep as our bellies for want of meat. (757)

After using a few more pages of *New England Trials,* Smith turned to Edward Winslow's *Good News from New-England,* published in London in the same year as the *Historie.* He summarized the whole of Winslow's book, omitting propaganda but moralizing a good deal, as when he added that an Indian who was hanged was "villainous." He next reprinted, from *New England Trials,* a borrowing from John Dee's *General and Rare Memorials* (1577). Following a final borrowing, from Richard Whitbourne's *Discourse Containing a Loving Invitation ... to ... the New found-land* (1622), Smith presented his own account of the state of affairs in New England, and a final bit of propaganda. Smith's hope was that fishing would now provide a sound economic basis for colonization, for fish "will afford as good gold as the mines of Guiana or Potassie, with less hazard and charge, and more certainty and facility" (784).

VIII The Historie Continued

Though Smith's reputation as a historian is considered to rest on the *Historie,* there is more continuous historical writing in the second part of the *True Travels* (1630), a continuation of the *Historie.* At first this part may appear to be mere padding, but Smith reported that, to prepare his accounts, he had "tired myself in seeking and discoursing with those returned" from America (884). He combined oral reports into a series of unified chapters that stress the growing prosperity of Virginia, the Bermudas, and New England.

Again Smith permitted himself personal touches. He chided the

Pilgrims, "whose humorous ignorance caused them, for more than a year, to endure a wonderful deal of misery, with an infinite patience, saying my books and maps were much better cheap to teach them than myself " (892). At times Smith's egotism is less attractive, as when he noted, bitterly, that "Those countries Captain Smith oft times used to call his children that never had mother, and well he might, for few fathers ever paid dearer for so little content" (893).

As narrative, the extension of the *Historie* on English activities in Guiana is particularly effective. Smith told with clarity and dispatch the little-known story, which began with Sir Walter Raleigh's work in 1595. Here Smith added a personal note: he was to have been a member of an expedition to Guiana in 1605; but, when the leader died, the voyage was not undertaken.

The story of the English colonies in the West Indies was Smith's next subject; his account seems to be based on written reports. But Smith had himself visited the isle of Nevis (he called it Mevis) in 1607, on his way to Virginia; and the description of that island is based on his recollection. The method of the *Historie* is suggested here by an apology, perhaps half ironic, that Smith felt obliged to make at this point: "Because I have ranged and lived amongst those islands, what my authors cannot tell me, I think it no great error in helping them to tell it myself" (909). Smith characteristically stretched the truth: he had spent just over two weeks in the West Indies.

IX The *Historie* Evaluated

The *Generall Historie* ends with no grand peroration. Indeed, it is difficult to know where it ends; for the continuation seems to conclude as an ending to the *True Travels* (with an invitation to read more of Smith's adventures in the *Historie*, here described as if it were another portion of the *Travels*). The original six books have no real ending, for the preparation of the *Historie*, especially that of the last pages, was hasty.[23] But Smith did plan a book on an impressive scale, and through the first three books the *Historie* is solid, carefully prepared.

While the book has been called Smith's "Memoirs, his Apologia, and his Defense,"[24] it was intended to be something more. The frustration and bitterness of half a lifetime apparently prevented Smith from preparing what he thought he would produce: a memorial collection to promote the colonies with which he felt so closely identified. From the evidence of the rest of the *Historie*, it appears that Book IV became the miscellany it is from personal

stitute Smith's chief claim to importance as historian (as distinguished from compiler) if the *Historie* is indeed Smith's greatest historical work.

Before the additions are examined, it will be helpful to consider the context of the preparation of the *Historie* in Smith's life. Since 1617 he had been an armchair adventurer, but a very impatient one. Smith believed that his experiences in Virginia had taught him how to control the Indians; and, after the massacre of 1622, he had sought in vain to have the Virginia Company send him with soldiers to subdue them. When he prepared the *Generall Historie,* in the forefront of his mind was the conviction that he alone knew how to deal with the Virginia Indians; he still hoped to go to Virginia to protect the English colonists. Many of the additions which he made to the 1612 account were motivated by these considerations.

I Smith's Additions

The first significant addition deals with an event which took place after Captain Newport and the ships which had delivered the colonists had departed. A second president had succeeded Wingfield, and Smith had been appointed supply officer with the task of seeking food for the hungry colonists. For this purpose, according to the 1612 version, "he went down the river to Kecoughtan, where at first they [the Indians] scorned him as a starved man, yet he so dealt with them that the next day they loaded his boat with corn" (96). The authors of "The Proceedings" apparently remembered the injunction of the London Virginia Company "not to offend the naturals" and thus preferred not to explain how Smith dealt with the Indians.

But since Smith was advocating after 1624 a tough Indian policy, one of the themes of Book IV, he wanted all to know how effectively he had frightened the Indians into submission in one of the earliest encounters. Smith's description, one of his most vivid pieces of prose, related how he had landed his men—only six or seven—and had advanced on the village, where quantities of corn could be observed. Then the Indians attacked:

Sixty or seventy of them, some black, some red, some white, some partly-colored, came in a square order, singing and dancing out of the woods, with their *Okee* (which was an idol made of skins, stuffed with moss, and painted and hung with chains and copper) borne before them; and in this manner, being well armed with clubs, targets, bows, and arrows, they charged the English, that so kindly received them with their muskets loaded with pistol-shot that down fell their god and divers lay sprawling on the ground. The rest fled again to the woods, and ere long sent one of their *Quiyoughkasouks* [priests] to offer peace and redeem their *Okee*. (393)

As in this passage, Smith often employed to good effect wry irony and lively pictures of his own heroism.

A few pages later occurs Smith's most famous addition in Book III, a two-thousand-word passage about his captivity which replaces a much briefer description in the earlier account. This anthology piece is presumably reprinted so often because of its substance: every American should have the opportunity to read Smith's classic account of his rescue by Pocahontas. Many readers must find the story quite different from what they had expected, for Smith made clear from the very beginning that it was his own behavior that had saved him, not Pocahontas. While he was a prisoner, "many strange triumphs and conjurations they made of him, yet he so demeaned himself amongst them as he not only diverted them from surprising the fort but procured his own liberty and got himself and his company such estimation amongst them that those savages admired him more than their own Quiyouchosucks" (395).

Smith saved himself by both bravery and quick-wittedness. As soon as he was captured, he asked to see the leader of the Indians; and he filled the chief with wonder and admiration by demonstrating his compass and by lecturing him on cosmology. Then he added to the impression that he was a wonder worker by revealing the magic of written communication: he asked that some Indians be sent to Jamestown with a message from him; and, when they saw what happened, they thought that Smith "could either divine or the paper could speak" (398). He also persuaded the Indians that an attack on Jamestown would be foolhardy since the settlers had huge guns and engines to guard them.

Smith's account emphasizes the savagery and the grotesqueness of the Indians. He told how he was the focus of fantastic ceremonies: "presently came skipping in a grim fellow, all painted over with coal, mingled with oil." "With most strange gestures and passions he began his invocation and environed the fire with a circle of meal; which done, three more such like devils came rushing in with the like antic tricks, painted half black, half red, but all their eyes were painted white, and some red strokes, like mustachios, along their cheeks. Round about him those fiends danced a pretty while, and then came in three more as ugly as the rest;

with red eyes and white strokes over their black faces" (398–99). When Smith was brought before Powhatan, the great chief, "more than two-hundred of these grim courtiers stood wondering at him, as if he had been a monster, till Powhatan and his train had put themselves in the greatest braveries" (399–400).

Smith made no effort to make his story suspenseful; instead, he showed that he was so valiant that he could see the comic side of the episode. Even the description of Pocahontas's intervention has an amusing touch, an anticlimax which takes something away from Pocahontas:

Two great stones were brought before Powhatan. Then as many as could laid hands on him, dragged him to them, and thereon laid his head, and being ready with their clubs to beat out his brains, Pocahontas, the king's dearest daughter, when no entreaty could prevail, got his head into her arms, and laid her own upon his to save him from death; whereat the emperor was contented he should live to make him hatchets, and her bells, beads, and copper, for they thought him as well of all occupations as himself. For the king himself will make his own robes, shoes, bows, arrows, pots; plant, hunt, or do anything as well as the rest. (400)

Perhaps Smith was being tested; perhaps Powhatan had arranged in advance for his daughter to rescue Smith. Responsible scholars have made these suggestions, but Smith said nothing. His concern was not really Pocahontas; it was Smith.[4]

Bradford Smith, the biographer of Captain Smith, devoted several pages of his study to conjectures as to why the rescue story did not appear in Smith's early and longer account of his captivity, the *True Relation* of 1608. Of course, one can only guess at the answer. Similarly, one can only conjecture as to Smith's reason for including it in the *Historie.* It may be here because one of Smith's special interests both in Book II, the reprinted "Description of Virginia," and in the additions to Book III is the relationship of the settlers and the Indians. It also served as a memorial treatment of Pocahontas, the dead wife of John Rolfe, whose bravery and devotion to the English Smith emphasized.

The next addition, one of about ninety words, also concerns the Indians; it points up Smith's care and watchfulness in preventing an Indian ambush when Captain Newport was to visit Powhatan. The passage (405) helps to create the impression that the Indians were a constant threat.

Otherwise only minor additions are to be noted for some pages after the captivity episode. The next long addition, about three hundred words, is—like the first—a story which emphasizes how

Smith and his men treated the Indians with severity. In exploring Chesapeake Bay, Smith and his men met Indians at a place called Cuskawaok. Though the Indians appeared innocent and peaceful, Smith suspected trouble: "there was nothing in them but villainy" (415). Once again Smith and his men, fourteen in number, went ashore, "discharging five or six shot among the reeds." The outcome was that the Indians recognized the superior force of the English, and they therefore "became such friends [that] they would contend who should fetch us water, stay with us for hostage, and gave us the best content" (415).

A few pages later (418), Smith added a good deal of information about a mine which he and his men had visited some ten miles inland from the Potomac. (The ore they obtained later proved worthless.) The purpose of the addition appears to have been to justify this exploring voyage: Smith somewhat defensively noted that they sought to determine the natural resources of the area. In similar fashion Smith added a few pages later (423–24) two paragraphs on geography, including a dozen or so place-name references not included in the original account. Some of these additions are slightly egotistical, such as the reference to "Willoughby's River," named for Smith's birthplace and Lord Willoughby, "his most honored friend."

By far the longest addition which Smith made to his source is a section of about thirty-three hundred words on the battles with the Rappahanocks and other Indians (424–32). "The Proceedings" reported simply that " . . . we had much wrangling of that peevish nation; but at last, they became as tractable as the rest" (119). In accounting for the change in attitude of the Indians, Smith wrote a lively story of four battles against Indians, all occasioned by treachery and ambushes. Some explanation of the pugnacity of the Indians was called for; and, with the capture of a wounded Indian (who was given careful medical assistance), an explanation was provided. He told them that the Indians had "heard we were a people come from under the world, to take their world from them" (427). Smith did not question the validity of the Indian's view, nor was he at all defensive in his characterization of his adventures. He conceived of the Indians as inferior peoples obliged to recognize the superior status of the English.[5] Mosco, an Indian guide who assisted the English in a variety of ways, was for Smith a childlike creature who took great delight in simple things: " . . . we contented Mosco in helping him to gather their arrows, which were an armful, whereof he gloried not a little" (427).

This long addition is thus part of the argument which was indirectly urged by means of the additions in Book III and directly urged in Book IV: send Smith with troops to subdue the Indians; force five hundred Indians to work for the maintenance of the settlers. Besides the Indian argument, Smith emphasized in Book IV—as has been noted above—the fruitfulness of the years when he served in Virginia in contrast to the more barren years that followed. In Book III this theme is not much apparent, except in the addition that Smith next made to his source. It is purportedly a letter which Smith sent to the Virginia London Company in reply to the instructions which Captain Newport had brought with him from London in September, 1608. Though it is presumably not, as Barbour noted, a verbatim copy, Moses Coit Tyler gave it an extended treatment as one of Smith's three American works.[6] (Probably the substance of the letter which Smith sent was much as one finds it in the *Generall Historie.*) There is reason to suppose that the London leaders took cognizance of what Smith wrote;[7] but, if the original was as belligerent in tone, it surely must have offended some people. It is truly one of Smith's most important writings, an extremely revealing document in vigorous prose.

Smith begins with a kind of courtesy not likely to win friends: " . . . I humbly entreat your pardons if I offend you with my rude answer" (442). Then Smith argued that, though he had concealed nothing from the Virginia Company, the Londoners were in no position to send detailed orders to the colonists since such instructions are inevitably unrealistic. Presumably, the London officials thought that conditions in Virginia were so favorable to exploitation that they deemed the insufficiency of the fruits of the first fifteen months of settlement to be the result of inactivity and lack of effort. The company had expected large, immediate efforts.

Smith answered the charges as a much unappreciated man. What do the Londoners know, he questioned, "but that [which] I have learned to tell you by the continual hazard of my life" (442). Again, recognition of his own bravery inspired Smith to irony: he bitterly noted how ridiculous it was to suppose that the exploration of the James River beyond the falls could be made in a barge transported around the barrier. If Newport "had burnt her [the barge] to ashes, one might have carried her in a bag, but as she is, five hundred cannot, to a navigable place above the falls" (443).

The chief source of the colony's troubles was, according to Smith, Captain Newport, whom he made the villain of Book III. As one of the first members of the Virginia governing council, admiral of the fleet that brought the first settlers to Virginia, and chief supplier of goods, food, and colonists from England, Newport had authority and prestige. But Smith noted that, according to rumor, Newport and many officials of the London Company "maintain their families out of that you send us" (444).

Smith's letter is a catalogue of explanations for the colony's failure to flourish: Newport, inadequate supplies, profiteering by the sailors of the supply ships, a lack of skilled labor. The document is remarkably self-confident. Smith had no doubts—either in late 1608 or in 1624, one supposes—that, if he could have had his way, the colony would have flourished. And his demands were not great.

Smith's self-confidence seems to have been the source of the many half-humorous remarks which make the letter attractive despite Smith's constant tone of irritation. Some of these remarks show that the Londoners were right in thinking the settlers to be lazy. "Though there be fish in the sea," wrote Smith, "fouls in the air, and beasts in the woods, their bounds so large, they so wild, and we so weak and ignorant, we cannot much trouble them" (444). (Smith's "we" is perhaps all of the colonists except Smith.) Captain Ratcliffe, a member of the governing council never very attractive to Smith, "is now called Sicklemore, a poor counterfeited imposture. I have sent him home, lest the company should cut his throat. What he is, now everyone can tell you" (444). Smith, one understands, had long known. This letter was an appropriate addition to Smith's source, for it does much to dramatize the plight of the colonists. It is one of the high points of the *Historie.*

Smith's next addition was also motivated by his desire to demonstrate the worth of his Indian policy. The passage of some two hundred twenty words (446–47) includes a paragraph on how Smith and his men learned to make camp in the woods in snowy weather.

The last extended addition made by Smith in preparing Book III is one of the most interesting, for it concerns Pocahontas. "The Proceedings" of 1612 had told the story of Smith's last visit with Powhatan and how Smith had bravely frustrated Powhatan's attempts to have him killed. For the *Historie,* Smith added three paragraphs, about three hundred words, to tell how Pocahontas, Powhatan's "dearest jewel and daughter," came in the "dark night" "through the irksome woods" to warn Smith of a new plot. The grateful captain sought to reward her, "but with the tears running down her cheeks, she said she durst not be seen to have any [gifts], for if Powhatan should know it, she were but dead, and so she ran away by herself, as she came" (455).

Since the Smith-Pocahontas legend is well known, one might suppose that the episode was added to fill out the picture of a relationship in which Smith took great pride. While there may have been something of this intention, in the context of Book III the reader of the account is more likely to find it part of Smith's effort to persuade the English to adopt his Indian policy. This Pocahontas episode shows that Smith's suspicion that the Indians were treacherous was well founded. (Smith added only one other reference to Pocahontas, and it was made in passing.)

II   Other Changes in the *Historie*

Besides these significant additions, all of which are effectively integrated into the narrative, Smith made many changes; and most of these are merely the result of responsible editing. Smith added geographical details, indicated what the later consequences of activities proved to be, made minor corrections, and added to lists of names. Some modifications reflect Smith's interests, for occasionally he added his name; and a number of small additions and changes were apparently motivated by egotism. For example, according to the 1612 account, the false charges against Smith had the effect of creating "a general hatred in the hearts of the company against unjust commanders" (93); according to Smith's revision, the consequences were also that Wingfield, the president, "was adjudged to give him [Smith] two hundred pounds, so that all he [Wingfield] had was seized upon in part of satisfaction, which Smith presently returned to the store for the general use of the colony" (389). Of all Smith's revisions, this one seems most likely to be fiction; for two hundred pounds would have been a huge fine. But, in fact, Wingfield himself reported this fine.[8] Smith's only inaccuracy was in dating: the incident occurred in September, when Wingfield was no longer president.

Many of the modifications are denigrations of Captain Newport, who, according to Smith's addition (440), wanted him deposed from his position as president. Smith criticized Newport's work as admiral: "we were at sea five months, where we both spent our victual and lost the opportunity of the time and season to plant, by the unskillful presumption of our ignorant transporters that understood not at all what they undertook" (392). The original version contains no such condemnation. Other changes make Smith seem very peevish. He omitted Newport's name when he referred to the presents sent to Powhatan.

1612 version	*1624 version*
Upon this Captain Newport sent his presents by water. (124)	Upon this, the presents were sent by water. (437)

Another change speaks for itself.

1612 version	*1624 version*
And Smith, to make clear these seeming suspicions that the savages were not so desperate as was pretended by Captain Newport, and how willing he was to further them to effect their projects, because the coronation would consume much time, undertook their message to Powhatan (to entreat him to come to Jamestown to receive his presents)	But Captain Smith, to make clear all these seeming suspicions that the savages were not so desperate as was pretended by Captain Newport, and how willing (since by their authority they would have it so) he was to assist them what he could, because the coronation would consume much time, he undertook himself their message to Powhatan, to entreat him to come to Jamestown to receive his presents. And where Newport durst not go with less than 120, he only took with
accompanied only with Captain Waldo, Master Andrew Buckler, Edward Brinton, and Samuel Collier. (123)	him Captain Waldo, Master Andrew Buckler, Edward Brinton, and Samuel Collier. (435–36)

On the other hand, Smith adds kind words about Thomas Wotton, the surgeon; George Percy; and John Coderington. And Smith modified his source a half dozen times to emphasize the virtues of his Indian policy.

The several speeches attributed to Smith are little changed. (To one, he added fifteen words.) Perhaps Smith had looked them over before their publication in 1612, but it seems very likely that Symonds, the editor, was primarily responsible for these Thucydidean orations. From time to time, Smith added passages which reflect his values, especially his piety (such as "God be thanked" and "God doth know"). At several points Smith supplemented the original list of authors of the narratives and added, apparently, himself to the list as "I.S." (403).

III   The *Historie* as History

One other consequence of Smith's additions is worth noting. Most of the new passages are lively narratives full of details about the forest, the landscape, and the Indians; full of action, often violent, these scenes are always vividly described. Smith's *Historie* has been read and admired because it brings the reader very close to the America of the first English settlers. In Book III his work is generally responsible, intelligent, and useful; but it is also one-sided and conditioned by Smith's very personal motives. Smith's additions to Book III are, however, important contributions to our knowledge of early Virginia; and the book makes very good reading today.

But Smith was a compiler, not a historian. To compare his work with that of William Bradford is to be unfair to Smith. He was much more like Hakuyt or Purchas; but, unlike these men, he dealt with what he knew firsthand (he was his own hero)—and he also added to the charm of his work the sense of his own attractive if opinionated personality.

CHAPTER 6

The Hack Writer

H AVING COMPLETED the *Generall Historie,* Smith could think of himself as a writer. The work he turned to next, *An Accidence, or The Pathway to Experience, Necessary for Young Sea-men,* was very successful in its time. It was not written from the motives that lie behind most of Smith's other writings; indeed, it seems to have been hack work. Besides, since it is not clear that Smith had a means of livelihood during the 1620's, he probably needed money such as he could earn from pamphleteering. He could still trade on the titles he had accumulated: "sometimes Governor of Virginia and Admiral of New England." (He had been in fact president of the governing council; later leaders were given the title of governor.) The *Accidence* and its sequel are the least important of Smith's writings, but some knowledge of the work and its composition contributes to an understanding of John Smith, man and writer.

I *An Accidence*

Smith seems to have gotten his idea for the *Accidence* from Gervase Markham's *Souldier's Accidence, or An Introduction to Military Discipline,* which appeared in 1625, the year before Smith's *Accidence.*[1] (The term *accidence* meant a discussion of the rudiments of a subject.) In the preface to Smith's forty-page quarto pamphlet—the first published seamen's manual in English—he explained his motives: since "many young gentlemen and valiant spirits do desire to try their fortunes at sea, I have been persuaded to print this discourse. ... " It was to serve, wrote Smith, "as an introduction for such as wants experience and are desirous to learn what belongs to a seaman" (787). Later, in the preface to the *True Travels,* Smith explained that his friend Sir Samuel Saltonstall had caused the book (or its augmented version) to be printed.

Smith was not a seaman, but his natural curiosity and practical bent must have led him to learn much from his extensive experiences at sea: in the Mediterranean, around Morocco, twice across the Atlantic, travels as a captive on a French ship off the Spanish and French coasts, exploring Chesapeake Bay—nearly a year and a half in all. From all this experience, he had learned the importance of a good diet at sea, something better than the usual dried fish, salted beef and pork, beer, oatmeal, cheese. In the *Accidence* he recommended that the food supply include currants, prunes and roasted beef packed in vinegar. He described with feeling the hard lot of a sailor, especially "after a storm, when poor men are all wet and some not so much as a cloth to shift him, shaking with cold" (804).

Most of the *Accidence* is little more than a series of lists: sails, winds, ropes, weapons. It is only occasionally that Smith captured the excitement of adventure at sea, as when he described terms of war in a bit of dialogue:

"The ship's on fire. Cut anything to get clear, and smother the fire with wet clothes."

"We are clear, and the fire is out, God be thanked."

"The day is spent. Let us consult. Surgeon, look to the wounded. Wind up the slain, with each a weight or bullet at his head and feet. Give three pieces for their funerals."

"Swabber, make clean the ship. Purser, record their names. Watch, be vigilant to keep your berth to windward and that we lose him not in the night. Gunners, sponge your ordnances. Soldiers, scour your pieces. Carpenters, about your leaks. Boats'n and the rest, repair the sails and shrouds. Cook, see you observe against the morning watch." (797)

Other passages here and there still make interesting reading, such as the list of duties of the marshal, who punishes offenders by "ducking at yardarms, hauling under the keel, bound to the capstern or mainmast with a basket of shot about his neck, setting in the bilboes ... (790).

Though intended to be practical, much of the *Accidence* is so condensed as to be almost unreadable, except perhaps to provide a vague, general impression of sea matters. Here, for example, is Smith's list of "the principal names of the timbers about the building [of] a ship":

First lay the keel, the stem and stern in a dry dock, or upon the stocks, and bind them with good knees. Then lay all the floor timbers, and cut your limber holes above the keel to bring the water to the well for the pump. Next your naval timbers, and bind them all with six-foot scarf at the least. The garbel strake is the outside plank next the keel. Be sure you have a good sufficient kelson, and then plank your outside and inside up, with your top timbers, but the lengths, breadths, depths, rakes, and burdens are so variable and different that nothing but experience can possibly teach. (792)

II *A Sea Grammar*

Smith noted in his preface, "For this small pamphlet, if you kindly accept it, I mean ere long more largely to explain the particulars" (788). The work was an immediate success, and Smith began work on an augmented version. Once again Smith borrowed his title from Gervase Markham, who had now prepared *The Soldiers Grammar*.[2] Smith called his new book, an eighty-eight page quarto pamphlet, which appeared in 1627, *A Sea Grammar, With The Plaine Exposition of Smiths Accidence for young Sea-men, enlarged.*

Philip L. Barbour has recently come to the conclusion that, soon after the publication of Smith's *Accidence*, someone called his attention to one of several manuscript copies then in circulation of Sir Henry Mainwaring's *Nomenclator Navalis*.[3] Mainwaring was an Oxford graduate of 1602 who turned to piracy and preyed on French and Spanish ships indiscriminately before receiving a royal pardon and being knighted in 1618. Not long thereafter he dedicated himself to writing a book for seamen in which he listed eight or nine hundred definitions of nautical terms. The earliest extant manuscript of this book was written between February, 1620, and February, 1623; but the most complete version dates from 1625.

Smith seems to have seen a copy of this version and to have availed himself of it for both convenience and accuracy. (Sir Henry was a seaman; Smith was not.) In using Mainwaring's manuscript (and it may have been unsigned) for reference, Smith borrowed many definitions verbatim or abbreviated them; he incorporated them into his original plan, that of the earlier *Accidence*. In short, *A Sea Grammar,* the new book, was a handbook, designed to be read; Mainwaring's was designed to be consulted. The latter was not published until 1644, when it appeared as *The Sea-mans Dictionary.* It was printed again twice, possibly three times. The *Sea Grammar* went through four later editions or reissues before 1700.[4]

Smith acknowledged within his text another borrowing, a long "philosophical speculation" on the question of how deep the sea is. This passage is very different from anything else in Smith's writings, for it is full of references to Plutarch, Pliny, Aristotle, and other authorities. Only at the end, with some reluctance, did Smith reveal his source: "If you desire any further satisfaction, read the first part of *Purchas His Pilgrimage,* where you may read how to find all those authors at large. Now because he hath taken near one hundred times as much from me, I have made bold to borrow this from him, seeing he hath sounded such deep waters for this ship to sail in, being a gentleman whose person I loved, and whose memory and virtues I will ever honor" (276). Both in his *Pilgrimage* and in his *Pilgrimes,* Purchas had published, as has been noted, excerpts from Smith; he had died in 1626.

The *Sea Grammar,* a much more impressive work than the *Accidence,* is much fuller and more professional, thanks in part to Mainwaring. The highly condensed account in the earlier version of how a ship is built gave way to a whole chapter that is clear and precise. But its competence does not increase its literary value. Only a chapter, an enlargement of the one quoted earlier on how to manage a sea fight, has much interest now. It is full of lively conversation.

III   Verses by Smith

Like several of Smith's other writings, the *Sea Grammar* is embellished with commendatory verses, seven in all. Such poems, labeled by Franklin B. Williams "metrical puffs,"[5] are frequently found in sixteenth- and seventeenth-century books. (One of the commendatory poems in the *Sea Grammar* is unusual in that it refers to the captain familiarly as "Jack Smith.") On two occasions Smith reciprocated with poems. Since he was thought to have written only one extant poem, "The Sea Marke," these two recently discovered poems are of considerable importance;[6] moreover, they show that Smith was a craftsman with considerable skill.

The earlier of these appeared in 1627 in *An Armado, or Navye, of 103 Ships & other Vessels; who have the art to Sayle by Land, as well as by Sea,* by John Taylor, a popular writer and famous London character, often known as the "water poet." Taylor's humorous pamphlet concerns such powerful "ships" as fellowship, courtship, and friendship. Taking his cue from Taylor, Smith used one dominant image in the poem. In mock-serious fashion, he warned the world of the danger occasioned by Taylor's fleet, so powerful that the gods of the sea, its monsters, and even the famous barriers such as Goodwin Sands off the coast of Kent are threatened. Among other aspects of Smith's art is his effective use of alliteration and sea terminology.

John Smith of his friend Master John Taylor and his Armado

Arm, arm, arm, arm, great Neptune, rouse, awake
And muster up thy monsters speedily.
Boreas unto thy blastering blasts betake;
Guard, guard yourselves, from Taylor's policy.
Rocks, shoals, lee-shores, oh help them, Goodwin sands,
For this new fleet runs over seas and lands,
And's now so victualed, rigged, and yarely plies,
It threatens all the waters, ayre and skies.
Truth in his navy such a power doth lead
The Devil, Hell, vice and all, the fleet may dreade.
And well it may, if well you understand,
So rare a fleet was never made nor manned.

In the *Accidence* and the *Sea Grammar* Smith recommended
to those interested in ships' guns "Master Robert Norton's exposi-
tions upon Master Digs." Earlier Norton had written a commendatory poem for the *Generall Historie* "to his much respected friend
Captain John Smith." (Taylor had not honored Smith in this fashion.) Now Smith reciprocated when Norton's *The Gunner* appeared in 1628. His poem is much less striking than the one he
had done the year before: it is full of the commonplaces of the
genre. But the often ungrammatical author of rough-hewn if vigorous prose did demonstrate with this poem that he was capable of
turning out for a fellow soldier something at least competent.

In the due Honor of the Author Master
Robert Norton, and his Work

Perfection, if't hath ever been attained,
In gunner's art, this author hath it gained
By study and experiences, and he
The fruit of all his pains hath offered thee,
A present well befitting this our age,
When all the world is but a martial stage.
Let sweeter studies lull asleep and please
Men who presume security, but these,
Thy labors practiced, shall more safely guard
Those that foresee the danger, th'other barred
This benefit. We soldiers do embrace
This rare and useful work, and o'r the face
Of all the world, let thy fame's echo sound

More than that roaring engine, and redound
To th'honor of our nation that thy pains
Transcends all former and their glory stains.

Captain John Smith,
Hungariensis.

CHAPTER 7

The Autobiographer

A HUNDRED YEARS ago Charles Deane and, more particularly the young Henry Adams tarnished John Smith's reputation as writer and historian. Deane, addressing scholars, questioned Smith's reliability as a historian. Adams, seeking to attract attention to himself, examined the Pocahontas story in a popular magazine and classified Smith as a liar. When in the 1890's Lewis Kropf, an amateur Hungarian historian, looked into Smith's account of his early years, the *True Travels*, he provided what appeared to be the ultimate condemnation of Smith's reliability. He doubted that Smith had ever been to eastern Europe, and he called the book "pseudo-romance."[1]

Until recently, Smith's *Travels* has as a consequence been much neglected. Countless popular articles have told the story of Smith's reputation, but even commentators on Smith's writings have had little to say about this story. The fullest account of Smith as a writer, that of Howard Mumford Jones, passes quickly by it, though Jones admires the work. Perhaps he might have said more, but, he noted, "Controversy will ever rage over the authenticity of the *True Travels*."[2]

In what seems to be the only other extended general account of Smith's writings in this century, the judicious Jarvis M. Morse carefully sidestepped the *True Travels*. Noting that the work is "partly fictitious," he argued that American scholars should not let doubts about it influence their judgment of Smith's other writings.[3] The classic work on early American literature, Moses Coit Tyler's *History of American Literature, 1607–1765*, says nothing about the *Travels;* for Tyler it was not an American book. But, thanks to the recent researches of Laura Striker, Bradford Smith, and especially Philip L. Barbour, Smith's account has been vindicated. Barbour's careful study led him to write that "nothing John Smith wrote has yet to be found to be a lie."[4]

I   Smith's Adventures

The True Travels, Adventures, and Observations of Captain John Smith, in Europe, Asia, Affrica, and America, from Anno Domini 1593 to 1629 appeared as a tall and handsome folio, decorated with illustrations, in 1630, the year before Smith's death. In this thin volume with only sixty pages of text, Smith set forth his adventures in France, Italy, Hungary, Turkey, Russia, and Morocco. Before an analysis of the book is undertaken, a brief summary may be helpful.[5]

Smith began the story of his youth with a few lines on his family, his home, and his limited education; then he plunged into his adventures, which began about his sixteenth year with brief visits to France and Scotland and "three or four years" of military service in the Netherlands. These years were but preparatory to his great adventure in the wars being fought in southeastern Europe, for which he started out in 1600, at the age of about twenty. (There was a lull in ·the fighting in the Netherlands.) Cheated of his money and his belongings in France, with only partially successful efforts at revenge, he was cast into the sea by a group of Catholic pilgrims who considered him a Jonah. "Yet God brought him to that little isle where was no inhabitants, but a few kine and goats. [Smith used the third person throughout.] The next morning, he espied two ships ... put in by the storm, that fetched him aboard, well refreshed him, and so kindly used him that he was well contented to try the rest of his fortune with them" (826).

Smith found himself on board a ship bound for Egypt, and he sailed along the African coast as far as Alexandria. On the return trip, Smith's ship engaged in a sea fight which led to adventures in the islands of the Mediterranean before he was finally able to reach Italy. Since all this time he was still headed towards the Hungarian wars, his passage appears to have been somewhat indirect. But Smith deliberately sought out new experiences to try his fortune, it appears, and so the time was not wasted.

Travels through Italy, mostly for sightseeing, preceded Smith's final arrival in Vienna. Becoming there a member of the army of the Holy Roman Empire, Smith soon made himself valuable by "an excellent strategem": he explained how widely separated troops could signal their intentions to one another by torches. After extended fighting, Smith demonstrated his abilities further, first by the use of elaborate pyrotechnics, then by defeating three Turks in a single combat.

After winning a captaincy on the field, Smith took part in a great battle in which the Turks were victorious: " ... Smith, among the slaughtered dead bodies, and many a gasping soul, with toil and wounds lay groaning among the rest, till being found by the pillagers, he was able to live; and perceiving by his armor and habit, his ransom might be better to them than his death, they led him prisoner with many others" (853).

He was sent to Istanbul to be the slave of the "fair mistress" of Bashaw Bogall. (Smith calls her "Charatza Trabigzanda." Though he thought this was her name, it simply means "girl from Trebizond.") She "took (as it seemed) much compassion for him." "But having no use for him, lest her mother should sell him, she sent him to her brother ... in Tartaria" (854). Extended descriptions of the Turks and Tartars fill several short chapters before one follows Smith to slavery north of the Black Sea and to his eventual escape up the Don to Muscovy. Finally Smith was able to return to Hungary through southern Poland. Having had his fill of battle, he toured Germany, France, Spain, and Morocco, the last mentioned being described in some detail. Once again he found himself in a sea fight, and once again he survived, finally returning to England after having been gone about four years. Here the story ends, for the second part of the *True Travels* is a continuation of Smith's *Generall Historie.* (See Chapters 4 and 8.) The book does not provide, as the title page promises, an account of Smith's adventures to 1629.

II   The Composition of the *Travels*

The strange nature and history of Smith's little book is not apparent from this summary or even from a careful reading. The place to begin an investigation would seem to be the dedicatory epistle, for in it Smith informs his reader that he wrote the story of his life which follows in response to a request by the antiquarian Sir Robert Cotton for "the whole course of my passages in a book by itself." In the writing of his autobiography, Smith is following, he reminded his readers, "many of the most eminent warriors and others; what their swords did, their pens writ." The book, Smith hopes, will "prevent ... all future misprisons" (808–9).

This account is in fact somewhat misleading if it suggests that the work is a new one. The basic story of Smith's life had appeared five years earlier, not as "a book by itself" but as a portion of the eighth book of *Purchas His Pilgrimes* (1625). The additions made for the 1630 version are the first chapter (a very condensed and rather obscure account of Smith's first twenty years), three chapters (XIV–XVI) on life in Tartary, and eleven chapters (XVIII–XXVIII) which contain little autobiographical material. Many details not appearing in the 1625 version are found in the later one; but the relationship of these two versions is far from clear, even if something can be said about it.

A further complication is that better than one-third of the earlier

version is said in the *Pilgrimes* to be extracts from an otherwise unknown work, *The Warres of Transilvania, Wallachi, and Moldavia,*
"written by Francisco Ferneza, a learned Italian, secretary to Sigismundus Bathor the Prince."[6] (This portion includes the story of
Smith's three successful jousts against Turkish opponents, by which
he won the right to embellish his shield with three Turks' heads.)
Smith repeated the attribution to Ferneza in the *True Travels* and
noted that Purchas had made the translation. In the dedication to
An Accidence, published in 1626, Smith recommended to those
curious about his life his own *Generall Historie* and *New Englands
Trialls,* and "The life of Sigismundus Bathor, Prince of Transylvania,
writ by his secretary, Francisco Ferneza" (788).

Just how Smith came to write the Purchas version is not known,
but presumably Purchas asked him for an account of his Near
Eastern adventures for inclusion in Book VIII of the *Pilgrimes,*
which deals with the Levant. What Smith supplied, Purchas probably trimmed and summarized in his usual fashion. Purchas may
also have suggested that Smith make use of Ferneza's *Warres* to
provide authenticity, since the version of Smith's story found in
the *True Travels* closely follows Ferneza's work as presented in
Purchas, much closer than the rest of the *Travels* follows Purchas.
(Smith's agreement to use Ferneza may have been made with the
proviso that Purchas follow Ferneza closely, but this is little more
than guesswork.) The problem of the composition of the *True
Travels* would be nearer solution were Ferneza's book extant.
Though some doubt that it ever existed, Smith's learned biogra-
pher Philip Barbour notes that no one has ever discovered that
Purchas invented a source.[7]

Smith wrote, according to my conjecture, an account of his life
for the *Pilgrimes,* from which Purchas trimmed a good deal and to
which Smith later added, in part by borrowing from other parts of
Purchas His Pilgrimes. The differences between the cut version of
Purchas and what is found in the *True Travels* can be seen by the
following parallel passages.

Purchas	*True Travels*
Opportunity casting him into the company of four French gallants well attended, faining to him	Opportunity casting him into the company of four French gallants well attended, faining to him the one to be a great lord, the rest his gentlemen, and that
they were devoted	they were all devoted

that way; over-persuaded him in the Low Countries, to go with them into France:	that way; over-persuaded him
	to go with them into France, to the Duchess of Mercury, from whom they should not only have means but also letters of favor to her noble Duke, then General to the Emperor Rodolphus in Hungary: which he did
with such ill weather as winter affordeth. (VIII, 321)	with such ill weather as winter affordeth. (823–4)

Both versions tell of Smith's being granted a pension for his services in fighting against the Turks—part of the portion from Ferneza. In the *True Travels* Smith supplied the patent by Sigmund Bathor authorizing his coat of arms and a certificate by an English official to the effect that he has seen the patent and recorded it in the Register of the College of Arms. Another portion appearing in both versions, a short passage, is a borrowing from William Biddulph, a description of the Turks' food to be found only a few pages before Smith's story in Purchas, though it had earlier appeared in *The Travels of Foure Englishmen* (London, 1612). Presumably Purchas, a friend of Smith's, brought Biddulph's account to Smith's attention.

III   Smith's Borrowings

Smith also augmented the earlier version by extensive borrowings, as Barbour has noted. Chapters XIV–XVI, life in Tartary, contain borrowings from two works found in the *Pilgrimes*: a thirteenth-century journal of Friar William of Rubruck, and Martin Broniovius's *Description of Tartaria*. A sample of Smith's borrowings follows:

Friar William	*Smith*
Their houses wherein they sleep, they ground upon a round foundation of wickers artificially wrought and compacted together: the roof whereof consisteth (in like sort) of wickers, meeting above into one little roundel, which roundel ascendeth upward a neck like unto a chimney, which they cover with white felt, and oftentimes they lay mortar or white earth upon the said felt, with the powder of	The princes houses are very artificially wrought, both the foundation, sides, and roof of wickers, ascending round to the top like a dove-cote; this they cover with white felt, or white earth tempered with the powder of

bones, that it may shine white. And sometimes also they cover it with black felt. The said felt on the neck of their house, they do garnish over with beautiful variety of pictures. Before the door likewise they hang a felt curiously painted over. For they spend all their colored felt, in painting vines, trees, birds, and beasts thereupon. *(Pilgrimes,* XI, 11.)	bones, that it may shine the whiter; sometimes with black felt, curiously painted with vines, trees, birds, and beasts. (587–88)

One wonders whether Smith found life in Tartary so little different from what Friar William found it that he could use an account almost four hundred years old. Perhaps the East was unchanging.

In writing the story of the Hungarian wars in which he was a participant, Smith used not only the aforementioned Ferneza but also Richard Knolles's *Generall Historie of the Turkes,* probably in the huge volume issued as the third edition in 1621. For the portion on Africa (Chapters XVIII-XIX) Smith used Hartwell's translation of Lopez and Pigafetta's *Report on the Kingdom of the Congo* (in *Purchas,* volume VI), and Robert Cottington's *Historie of Barbarie* (in *Purchas,* volume VI). These borrowed sections, like the one quoted above, are mostly descriptive of strange places and peoples.

Smith referred to some of these sources, as when he advised his reader, "Of all these you may read in the history of this Edward Lopez, translated into English by Abraham Hartwell, and dedicated to John, Lord Archbishop of Canterbury, 1597" (877). On another occasion, after borrowed descriptions of life in Tartary, Smith prepared his readers for more borrowings, but these are not supplied. "Many other most strange and wonderful things are in the land of Cathay towards the North-east, and China towards the South-east, where are many of the most famous kingdoms in the world; where most arts, plenty, and curiosities are in such abundance, as might seem incredible, which hereafter I will relate, as I have briefly gathered from such authors as have lived there" (865). Smith had touched Asia only at the Bosphorus. If we reduce the *True Travels* to autobiographical portions that Smith seems to have written himself, we end up with a work of only about twelve thousand words.

IV   An Evaluation

Edward Arber, Smith's editor and an authority on sixteenth- and early seventeenth-century English literature, said of the *True Travels,* "in its clear, graphic, and condensed style, the narrative is among the very best written English books of travel printed in Smith's lifetime" (xxv). To the reader of contemporary travel writing, such as that in *Purchas,* this praise seems somewhat excessive. Smith's style is often far from clear because it is so condensed, and many of the most graphic passages are borrowed. John Gould Fletcher's comment is more valid: Smith's "literary style is, at best, the brief campaign-notes of a blunt soldier."[8] Smith truly did not always tell his story well, and he lost immediacy by using the third person to refer to himself. Perhaps he followed the example of Julius Caesar, whose writings Smith obviously knew. Like Caesar, he told nothing of his personal reactions to what he saw and did, but his descriptions are nevertheless vivid enough to permit one sometimes to picture his actions. Thus, after having been captured by the Turks, enslaved, and shipped to what is now southern Russia,

... he became a thresher at a grange in a great field, more than a league from the tymor's [correctly *timariot*—a captain] house. The bashaw [for *bashi,* captain] as he oft used to visit his granges, visited him; and took occasion so to beat, spurn, and revile him, that forgetting all reason, he beat out the tymor's brains with his threshing bat, for they have had no flails; and seeing his estate could be no worse than it was, clothed himself in his [the bashi's] clothes, hid his body under the straw, filled his knapsack with corn, shut the doors, mounted his horse, and ran into the desert at all adventure. (866)

Some of Smith's adventures are described in much less vivid language; some descriptions are so abbreviated as to be almost meaningless. Other passages are little more than catalogues. Thus Smith led up to his service in the Hungarian wars with this summary:

Returning by Capua, Rome, and Siena, he passed by that admired city of Florence, the cities and countries of Bologna, Ferrara, Mantua, Padua, and Venice, whose gulf he passed from Malamoco and the Adriatic Sea for Ragouza, spending some time to see that barren coast of Albania and Dalmatia, to Capo de Istria, traveling the main [land] of poor Slavonia by Lubbiano [Ljublana] till he came to Graz in Styria, the seat of Ferdinando, Arch-duke of Austria, now Emperor of Almania: where he met an Englishman and an Irish Jesuit; who acquainted him with many brave gentlemen of good quality, especially with the Lord Ebersbaught. (828)

On the other hand, it must be said that the borrowings are intelligently made and that they usually add to the interest of the work. (Since the *Generall Historie* is mainly a compilation, Smith was an experienced borrower.) The adventures themselves are frequently so exciting that the work is interesting despite Smith's failings as a writer. The book provides a picture of Smith as a

dashing and intrepid adventurer whose ingenuity was a great as-
set to his Hungarian colleagues and on occasion saved his life.
Only once is Smith shown to be anything but a man of action.
Here is our autobiographer at the age of twenty, gathering his
resources and adding to them after several years of warfare in the
Netherlands and travels in France and Scotland:

... being glutted with too much company, wherein he took small delight,
he retired himself into a little woody pasture, a good way from any town,
environed with many hundred acres of other woods. Here by a fair brook
he built a pavillion of boughs, where only in his clothes he lay. His study
was Machiavelli's *Art of War,* and Marcus Aurelius; his exercise a good
horse, with his lance and ring; his food was thought to be more of venison
than anything else; what he wanted, his man brought him. The country
wondering at such an hermit, his friends persuaded one Signore
Theodora Palaloga [Paleologue], rider to Henry, Earl of Lincoln, an excellent horse-man and a noble Italian gentleman, to insinuate into his wood-
ish acquaintaines; whose languages and good discourse, and exercise of
riding, drew him to stay with him at Tattersall. (823)

Since Smith was an experienced and on occasion an effective
writer by the time he wrote the story of his youth, as the passage
just quoted demonstrates, it is a pity that he did not take greater
care with his *True Travels.* Yet the book has remarkable qualities.
It is surely striking that Smith could report with considerable accuracy where he had been, though he wrote from memory nearly
twenty-five years after the events, without the aid of notes or a
journal, without much knowledge of foreign languages—some Italian, probably a fair knowledge of French, and a little German—
and with only the typical maps of his day, thoroughly inadequate
ones, to jog his memory. (He does seem, however, to have picked
up some help from books and maps.)

Though the literary quality of the *True Travels* is not consistently high, the adventures themselves still may charm readers as
Othello's "hairbreath 'scapes" charmed Desdemona (and they
have the advantage of being true). Obviously, they were valuable
experiences for John Smith, who won his title of captain (of 250
horse) in Hungary. (He was later made major, but he seems to
have preferred the title of captain.) As he wrote in his last work,
Advertisements For the unexperienced Planters of New England
(1631), "The wars in Europe, Asia, and Africa taught me how to
subdue the wild savages in Virginia and New England, in
America" (925). He could call himself an English gentleman, too;
that is what Bathor's document calls him. Smith's story tells how

he became self-reliant, tough, a leader of men, experienced in warfare. Having made himself valuable, he would not have to wait long to put his well-developed talents to work in Virginia, where once again he would achieve status despite his blood and his education.

Though he waited until near the end of his life to tell his story, Smith made interesting use of aspects of his early adventures in his American explorations. In a voyage up Chesapeake Bay, he named a peninsula Point Ployer after a French nobleman who had befriended him in Brittany, and in his New England travels he named a "fair headland" Cape Tragabigzanda after the girl whose slave he had been in Istanbul, and three islands off the headland Three Turks' Heads. Later Smith presented his map of New England (the most elaborate until then by far) to Prince Charles (later Charles I) with the request that he change the "barbarous" Indian place names for "such English, as Posterity may say, Prince Charles was their Godfather" (177). Charles changed Cape Trabigzanda to simple Ann, for his mother; and posterity, ignoring Smith's exploits, soon gave the islands individual names: Thatcher, Milk, and Straitsmouth. (They are not to be confused with T. S. Eliot's "Dry Salvages" or Trois Sauvages.)

Smith himself characterized his career best: "how oft up, how oft down, sometimes near despair, and ere long flourishing" (944). Both recognition and disparagement have since his death been the story of his reputation. Though all the facts can never be known, modern scholarship permits a sound assessment of Captain John Smith, his life and writings. To make the assessment, one must understand that peculiar autobiography, the *True Travels*.

CHAPTER 8

The New England Writings

B ECAUSE everyone knows the story of Pocahontas and because Smith's *magnum opus* is often referred to as the *Generall Historie of Virginia*, Captain John Smith is seldom identified with New England. Yet he gave it its name; and, as no less an authority than Samuel Eliot Morison emphasized, Smith was "for long the principal promoter of her settlement."[1] From 1614 to 1631, when he died, Smith devoted himself largely to the colonizing of New England. The theme of three of his works is New England, and one of these is his best.

I *A Description of New England*

Englishmen had shown little interest in New England before 1602. (The story of the voyage of that year and later English visits to the area is discussed in Chapter I, and by Smith himself in Book I of the *Generall Historie*.) Smith visited New England only once, in 1614; and he stayed only three months. He explored the Maine and Massachusetts coasts; the story of this visit forms the basis of Smith's third publication, *A Description of New England* (1616). Smith wrote this seventy-nine page quarto during the summer and fall of 1615, while a captive on board a French ship. (Smith had been trying to return to America when he was captured.) Under these strange circumstances, "to keep my perplexed thoughts from too much meditation of my miserable estate, I writ this discourse ... " (224).

The importance of this little book is great because of its historical consequences and its crucial role in Smith's career as a writer. Of the latter, Philip Barbour writes that, with this propaganda pamphlet, Smith "found his true métier."[2] Of the former, Henry F. Howe argues that "neither Pilgrims nor Puritans would have reached Massachusetts when they did had it not been for Smith and his *Description of New England*. His was indeed the signal individual achievement in the founding of Massachusetts."[3]

Smith, who sought to make his pamphlet as impressive as possible for propaganda purposes, dedicated it to Prince Charles, who had agreed to provide English names for the Indian ones on the excellent map of the area which accompanied the text. (Only three of Charles's names survive: Cape Ann, the Charles River, and Plymouth.) Smith also addressed prefatory epistles to the King's Privy Council and to the companies of adventurers in London, Bristol, Exeter, and wherever; and he saw to it that nine poems, including ones by George Wither and by John Davies, precede and follow the text.

From these poems and prefaces comes an image of Smith which inevitably affects one's reading of the tract. From the poems it appears that Smith was the victim of envy and malice, though a world-traveling patriot, the hero of Virginia, a thoroughly honorable man. A former subordinate in arms wrote: "I never knew a warrior yet but thee/ From wine, tobacco, debts, dice, oaths so free" (231). A friend and relative, Nicholas Smith, wrote,

> "Hence damned Detraction: stand not in our way.
> Envy itself will not the Truth gainsay" (182).

In the preface Smith describes himself as the author of "this rude discourse," ready to expose his "imbecility to contempt." He excuses himself for having been captured by pirates: "four men of war, provided as they were, had been sufficient to have taken Samson, Hercules, and Alexander the Great ... " (179–80). From this time on, most of Smith's writings constantly remind the reader that he was a true hero victimized by circumstances.

The miscellaneous nature of Smith's book is suggested by its full title: *A Description of New England: or The Observations, and discoveries, of Captain John Smith (Admirall of that Country⁴) in the North of America, in the year of our Lord 1614: with the successe of sixe Ships, that went the next yeare 1615; and the accidents befell him among the French men of warre: With the proofe of the present benefit this Countrey affoords; wither this present yeare, 1616, eight voluntary Ships are gone to make further tryall.* The framework is basically chronological, but it is loose enough to permit Smith to include propaganda, specific suggestions concerning colonization, philosophizing, comments on his map and his values, and a document providing information about Smith's unsuccessful voyage of 1615. Some of Smith's best writing was occasioned by the enthusiasm with which he contemplated the colonization of New England. His frustration at his inability to be developing a colony there himself led him to pour his energies into writing.

The prose of the *Description* is often quite different from anything found in Smith's earlier works. For example, in his efforts to stir his readers to recognize the virtues of colonies, he wrote the following artful passage of a decidedly philosophical cast.

Consider: what were the beginnings of the monarchies of the Chaldeans, the Syrians, the Grecians, and the Romans, but this one rule—What was it they would not do for the good of the commonwealth or their mother city? For example, Rome. What made her such a monarchess but only the adventures of her youth, not in riots at home but in dangers abroad, and the justice and judgment out of their experience when they grew aged? What was their ruin and hurt but this: the excess of idleness, the fondness of parents, the want of experience in magistrates, the admiration of their undeserved honors, the contempt of true merit, their unjust jealousies, their politic incredulities, their hypocritical seeming goodness, and their deeds of secret lewdness. ... Then who would live at home idly (or think in himself any worth to live) only to eat, drink, sleep, and so die? Or by consuming that carelessly [which] his friends got worthily? Or by using that miserably that maintained virtue honestly? ... Or (to maintain a silly show of bravery) toil out thy heart, soul, and time basely, by shifts, tricks, cards, and dice? (209)

Nothing in Smith's earlier writing prepares the reader for the rhetorical flourishes,—the alliteration, the parallel constructions, the richness—of this passage.

Despite his moralistic approach, with its emphasis on hard work, honesty, and patriotism, Smith is fundamentally materialist and bourgeois. He has much to say about the opportunity to get rich in the New World. "I am not so simple to think," wrote Smith, "that ever any other motive than wealth will ever erect there a commonwealth" (212). His later impatience with the Pilgrims perhaps stemmed from the fact that their religious motives did not fit his expectations. Elsewhere in the *Description* Smith did invoke religion as a motivation for colonization, but in their context the words ring hollow: "Religion, above all things, should move us (especially the clergy) if we were religious to show our faith in our works in converting those poor savages to the knowledge of God, seeing what pains the Spaniards take to bring them to their adulterated faith"(217).

Besides patriotism, wealth, and religion, Smith suggested another motive for going to New England: it was a pleasant place to live, his preferred place, where everyone, young or old, rich or poor, could be happy. A gentleman might have all the pleasures which hawking and hunting provide, and for the ordinary workman, "What pleasure can be, more than (being tired with any occasion ashore, in planting vines, fruits, herbs, in contriving their own grounds, to the pleasure of their own minds, their fields, gardens, orchards, buildings, ships, and other works, etc.) to recreate themselves before their own doors, in their own boats upon the seas, where man, woman, and child with a small hook and line, by angling, may take divers sorts of excellent fish at their pleasures?" (213). Smith's insistent emphasis on *own* is not to be ignored; he was clearly a propagandist. (One wishes that Smith's admiration of the climate of New England, another subject to which he gives special attention, could have undergone the test of a typical winter; for his visit was in late spring and summer.)

Smith was inconsistent in his discussion of the motives for colonization, but the many virtues of the book more than outweigh its occasional aimlessness. Smith's visit to New England had been a brief one, yet he was able to provide a precise description of the coastline both in the *Description* and on the map (no easy feat, as other descriptions and maps of the time demonstrate); the Indian names or his own for the most important topographical features; and a very full list of the flora and fauna, including what seems to be the first mention of the muskrat by a visitor to New England. Whereas earlier colonizing efforts had been directed at Maine, he saw that Massachusetts was the best place in New England for settlement; to him, it was "the paradise of all those parts" (204).

Most of Smith's descriptions of the coast, Indian tribes, wildlife, and vegetation consist of little more than a catalogue. At times, however, Smith offers charming pictures, such as these:

... I made a garden upon the top of a rocky isle in 43½ [degrees], four leagues from the main[land], in May, that grew so well as it served us for sallets in June and July. (198) Angoam [Agawam] is the next. This place might content a right curious judgment, but there are many sands at the entrance of the harbour, and the worst is, it is embayed too far from the deep sea. Here are many rising hills, and on their tops and descents, many corn fields and delightful groves. (204)

. . . . . .

[There is] no river where there is not plenty of sturgeon or salmon or both, all which are to be had in abundance, observing but their seasons. But if a man will go at Christmas to gather cherries in Kent, he may be deceived, though there be plenty in summer. So here, these plenties have their season, as I have expressed. (207–08)

Smith was not only an excellent explorer; he was also a thoughtful creator of seemingly sound and certainly concrete proposals for colonization. E. G. R. Taylor asserts that "Nothing could be more judicious than Smith's proposals for organized settlement" of

New England.[5] Smith knew from his Virginia experience that "it is not a work for everyone, to manage such an affair as makes a discovery and plants a colony." He knew that it required "all the best parts of art, judgment, courage, honesty, constancy, diligence, and industry to do but near well"; that "Some are more proper for one thing than another, and therein are to be employed"; and that "nothing breeds more confusion than misplacing and misemploying men in their undertakings" (191).

Smith's specific plan for colonization depended on his presence in America. It called for him to be provided with two groups of men to start a colony: soldiers to control the Indians, who may be warlike "because of the abuses which have been offered them";[6] and experienced and skilled workmen, who can teach the skills needed in the new land. Smith sought in particular: "carpenter, mason, gardener, tailor, smith, sailor, forger".(213)

With this nucleus, the colony could accept each year many unskilled laborers who would work their way to America on fishing ships by assisting with the fishing until the ships were loaded. Then, Smith proposed, "their ships returning, leave such [laborers] with me, with the value of that they should receive coming home, in such provisions and necessary tools, arms, bedding, and apparel, salt, hooks, nets, lines, and such like, as they spare of the remainings." These laborers "till the next return may keep their [the fishermen's] boats and do them many other profitable services" (199–200). Smith thought that poor people, including children, could be advantageously shipped to America to serve as laborers. (Many Londoners considered that plagues were caused by conditions among the poor, and in 1617 five hundred pounds was raised to ship one hundred poor children to Virginia, where they were to be apprenticed until the age of fifteen.[7])

Smith's account specified the profits to be realized from fishing and offered ideas on later improvements of the arrangement. The process would, in Smith's opinion, result in substantial immediate profits; but patience would be required for real success. As Smith puts it in one of his most effective passages,

... if twenty years be required to make a child a man, seven years limited [to] an apprentice for his trade; if scarce an age be sufficient to make a wise man a statesman, and commonly a man dies ere he hath learned to be discreet; if perfection be so hard to be obtained as of necessity there must be practice as well of theoric, let no man much condemn this paradox opinion, to say that half seven years is scarce sufficient for a good capacity to learn in these affairs how to carry himself, and whoever shall try in these remote places the erecting of a colony shall find at the end of seven years occasion enough to use all his discretion, and hopes will be necessarily required. ... (215–16)

This passage continues on luxuriantly, at times all but getting out of hand, as Smith piles up strings of nouns and clauses.

On the basis of his own experienced leadership—he who had "learned there is a great difference betwixt the directions and judgment of experimental knowledge and the superficial conjecture of variable relation" (218)—Smith believed he could make a successful colony with soldiers and workmen. As he conceived it, the social structure of the colony would differ in significant ways from that of the mother country; for America would permit the development of the self-made man. "Who can desire," he wrote, "more content that hath small means or but his own merit to advance his fortune, than to tread and plant that ground he hath purchased by the hazard of his life?" (208)[8] "And here are no hard landlords to rack us, with high rents or extorted fines to consume us" (196).

In 1615 Smith was given the opportunity to do what he had in mind; but, after having had his would-be colonists reduced to a mere sixteen, his plans were, as has been noted, interrupted by pirates, to Smith's immense irritation and embarrassment. *A Description of New England* ends with an account of these misadventures which includes one of Smith's most vivid pictures of himself. For months he had been held captive by French pirates; now on board ship in a French port,

... in the end of such a storm that beat them all under hatches, I watched my opportunity to get ashore in their boat, whereinto, in the dark night, I secretly got, and with a half pike that lay by me, put adrift for Rat Isle, but the current was so strong and the sea so great, I went adrift to sea, till it please God the wind so turned with the tide that although I was, all this fearful night of gusts and rain, in the sea the space of twelve hours, when many ships were driven ashore, and divers split (and being with sculling and bailing the water tired, I expected each minute would sink me), at last I arrived in an oozy isle by Charowne [Charente], where certain fowlers found me near drowned and half dead with water, cold, and hunger. (226)

The passage is typical of Smith: confused sentence construction that still does not prevent the experience from being realized in words.

Smith then briefly told the story of his return to England and concluded with a final exhortation to himself and his readers to overcome their "idleness and ingratitude to all posterities, and the neglect of our own duties in our piety and religion we owe our God, our King, our country" (229).

An additional page inserted in some copies of the pamphlet lists the Indian place names or new ones supplied by Smith, and in a second column the ones which Prince Charles had substituted. For Cape Tragabigzanda, Charles substituted Anna, his mother's name. The former name was not Indian but one with which Smith memorialized the girl who had befriended him in Constantinople, where he had been a Turkish captive in 1603. (See the account of the *True Travels* in Chapter 7.) Smith's pamphlet appeared in only one separate edition, but the map was frequently reprinted, and he incorporated the *Description* into Book VI of the *Generall Historie.*

Smith's most important contributions to American place names deserve special mention. Thoughout his pamphlet, Smith referred to the area he had visited as *New England.* It had formerly been called *the northern part of Virginia* or *Norumbega;* but Smith's *Description* and his map, with Prince Charles's confirmation, gave it the name it still has.[9] Smith did not invent the name *Massachusetts,* but he picked up the name of the Indian tribe and used it for the region now called by the name, or rather the portion of the region near what is now Boston.[10]

II *New Englands Trials*

Smith continued to seek to establish a colony in America. In 1617, probably under the auspices of the North Virginia Company, he prepared to cross the Atlantic with three ships; but he was again frustrated. Contrary winds kept the ships from leaving Plymouth harbor; and, after three months' delay, the voyage was abandoned. Smith's title—Admiral of New England—proved to be painfully ironic, for he never went to sea again.

The year after this frustration, 1618, Smith wrote to Lord Bacon to request a five-thousand-pound investment for the pet project of a colony in New England.[11] Again his plans called for profits from fishing. Though no colonists had arrived in America since Smith's 1614 voyage, Englishmen were enjoying good profits from fishing expeditions off the coast; he cited a good deal of evidence. This time he described his 1614 voyage as a financial success, though, according to his 1616 report, it is not clear that it had been. Achieving no results with this letter, Smith decided to revise and publish it in order to appeal to other possible sponsors. It appeared in late 1620. He called the brief pamphlet *New Englands*

Trials. Declaring the successe of 26. Ships employed thither within these sixe yeares: with the benefit of that Countrey by sea and land: and how to build threescore sayle of good ships, to make a little Navie Royall (1620). (By trials, Smith meant proofs.)

This promotional tract he presented, according to the *Generall Historie,* "with a great many maps both of Virginia and New England . . . to thirty of the chief companies of London at their halls, desiring either generally or particularly (them that would) to embrace it, and by the stock of five thousand pounds to ease others of the superfluity of most of their companies that had but strength and health to labor" (748). As Wilberforce Eames has shown in his Smith bibliography, copies were addressed to "the Right Honorable Adventurers to all discoveries and planations, especially to New England," to the company of fishmongers (and presumably other guilds), to Chief Justice Edward Coke, and to Sir John Egerton.[12] Again Smith found no backers.

The first edition of *New Englands Trials* is a collection of very miscellaneous materials. After a brief introduction on New England's location, geography, and climate, Smith presented statistics on the profits which have been made from fishing. Then he noted the advantages of New England for fishing and cited ten proofs of these advantages in the form of brief factual reports on successful fishing voyages. Then comes an autobiographical passage. Smith's sense of mistreatment and neglect, reflected in the prefaces and poems of *A Description of New England,* is in the background of the text of that work; in *New Englands Trials* it comes to the foreground.

Having cited the virtues of New England and the successful fishing ventures made there, Smith felt obliged to face the question of why he himself had done so little. Why did he make "no more use of it and rest so long without employment?" (242). Smith answers by reporting his great sacrifices of time and money on behalf of both Virginia and New England. With great bitterness he reports, "I never had power and means to do anything (though more hath been spent in formal delays than would have done the business) but in such penurious and miserable manner, as if I had gone begging to build an university, where, had men been as forward to adventure their purses as to crop the fruits of my labors, thousands ere this had been bettered by these designs" (243). In the earlier book on New England, the autobiographical aspect was appropriate. Smith was, after all, describing what he uniquely knew. But his zeal to colonize the New World was marred by his inability to subordinate his own disappointment.

vides few facts about Smith which he had not set forth alread[y]
the personality of the author shines through more attractively
anywhere else. A. L. Rowse has argued that Smith "is a write[r]
nature: the very assertion of personality shows it, against [all]
dogs."[14] But elsewhere Smith's writings are not always *enlivened* [by]
a sense of the author's personality. Indeed, when Smith injected h[is]
personality, he too often marred his work with his tone of the victimized hero. The *Advertisements,* though fuller of braggadocio than
any of Smith's other works, shows much more of the spirit which was
revealed at points in the second part of the *True Travels:* a sense of
his own triumph and success. Here is his outlook, vigorously expressed:

Having been a slave to the Turks, prisoner amongst the most barbarous
savages, after my deliverance commonly discovering and ranging those
large rivers and unknown nations with such a handful of ignorant compan-
ions that the wiser sort oft gave me [up] for lost; always in mutinies, wants,
and miseries, blown up with gunpowder; a long-time prisoner among the
French pirates, from whom escaping in a little boat by myself and adrift all
such a stormy winter night—when their ships were split, more than a
hundred thousand pound lost they had taken at sea and most of them
drowned upon the isle of Ré, not far from whence I was driven on shore
in my little boat, etc. And many a score of the worst of winter months lived
in the fields, yet to have lived near thirty-seven years in the midst of wars,
pestilence, and famine, by which many an hundred thousand have died
about me, and scarce five living of them [that] went first with me to Virginia, and yet see the fruits of my labors thus well begin to prosper. Though
I have but my labor for my pains, have I not much reason both privately
and publicly to acknowledge it and give God thanks, whose omnipotent
power only delivered me, to do the utmost of my best to make his name
known in those remote parts of the world and his loving mercy to such a
miserable sinner. (945)

This passage reveals a great deal about Smith. Once he has worked
his way through the syntax, the reader is struck by the romanticized
or exaggerated view of himself which Smith had developed in the
fifteen years since his last real adventure. The passage also shows
that Smith's imagination offered him considerable consolation and
comfort in his pain and bitterness. It also reveals Smith's new appreciation of the importance of religion, which also seems to have
provided him with consolation. This impression is strengthened by
the fact that the *Advertisements* was dedicated to the Archbishops
of Canterbury and York, "to leave testimony to the world how highly
I honor as well the miter as the lance" (920).

This flaw marks both *New Englands Trials* and the *Generall Historie.* It was ironic, therefore, for Smith to complain of "everyone so
regarding his private that it is hard to effect public good" (243–
44).

Smith next urged his colonizing plan, which was what it had
been, to combine fishing expeditions with colonizing. To this end,
Smith suggested that Britain had had an historic interest in fishing. His authority was John Dee's *General and Rare Memorials*
(1577), which Smith referred to as the *British Monarchy.* He used
almost everything else that came to hand with little sense of dis-
crimination or plan: geographical description, catalogues of fish,
requests for funds, quotations. The 1620 version is not marked by
any particular literary excellence; indeed, it seems to have been
hastily thrown together.

A second edition of *New Englands Trials* was prepared in October, 1622, and published soon after with dedications to Prince
Charles and to the adventurers. This edition added to the first an
account of recent events. It is half again as long as the first edition, fourteen pages to the first edition's eight. The 1622 version
contains interesting new material, but it too seems patched
together. Smith added three paragraphs on the Plymouth Colony,
its adventures and misadventures, set forth in a simple and factual
manner, though he did not deny himself the opportunity of men-
tioning that the colonists were "for want of experience ranging to
and again six weeks before they found a place they liked to dwell
on" (260). (Had he guided them, they would have had no problems.) Later he was to chide them for seeking "to save charges"
by trying "their own conclusions, though with great loss and misery" (941). They considered, he wrote, "my books and my maps
... much better cheap to teach them than myself" (892). Smith
also included in the 1622 edition a letter confirming his report on
the wealth of New England in foodstuffs. This letter made an
observation which Smith frequently emphasized: the colonies
need not be encumbered with the English social structure. "We
are all freeholders," wrote William Hilton; "the rent day doth not
bother us" (261).

Another letter from New England, reporting that the colonists
there were "more wary" of the Indians since the massacre in
Virginia in March, 1622, led Smith to an extended and significant
digression—eight paragraphs on Virginia which could be considered propaganda on his own behalf. When Smith rehearsed his
experiences with Virginia Indians, his writing came alive. He reported on his prowess as military leader and Indian fighter.

"When I had ten men able to go abroad, our commonwealth was very strong. With such a number I ranged that unknown country fourteen weeks. I had but eighteen to subdue them all, with which great army I stayed six weeks before their greatest king's habitation, till they had gotten all the power they could" (262).

Smith had already proposed earlier in 1622 that he be put in charge of a group of soldiers to prevent further massacres. Later, in the *Generall Historie,* he told the story of his offer and the neglect which it met. Yet now he felt that, despite the lack of recognition which his efforts brought him, he might still speak of the American colonies as "my children, for they have been my wife, my hawks, my hounds, my cards, my dice, and in total my best content" (265). He wanted very much to return. This digression also includes Smith's first published account of his rescue by Pocahontas. (In the *Generall Historie* he was to include a letter about how she had saved him; this letter he dated from 1616.) Here he wrote merely that, when the Indians had captured him, "God made Pocahontas, the king's daughter, the means to deliver me" (263).

The enlarged *New Englands Trials* is still very slight; and, except for the autobiographical passage, its literary value is not great. Historically, the pamphlet is more important; for it provides a full record of English voyages to New England from 1616 to 1622. Smith's careful distribution of copies of the pamphlet presumably did something towards directing English attention to New England. (The first edition, it should be noted, did not appear until after the Pilgrims had departed.)

III   New England in the *Generall Historie*

In the *Generall Historie* Smith reprinted in slightly revised form his two earlier writings on New England and abridgments of other men's writings. (See the discussion in Chapter 5.) He also added a few comments, such as a paragraph on the comparative worth of gold and silver mines and of fish. The continuation of the *Generall Historie,* published as the second part of the *True Travels* (1630), includes an important chapter on "The proceedings and present state of New England since 1624 to the present 1629." This chapter is more strictly autobiographical than *New Englands Trials.* Throughout its survey of the recent history of New England, one is never permitted to forget whose voice is behind the words.

Smith began by emphasizing that, before his 1614 visit, New England was "then reputed by your westerlings [the Plymouth Company] a most rocky, barren, desolate desert, but [from] the

good return I brought from thence, with the maps and relations I made of the country, which I made so manifest, some of them did believe me." While some voyages were made to New England, Smith was "fed ... with delays, promises, and excuses, but no performance of anything to any purpose" (891). It is only too apparent that Smith bitterly resented this treatment, especially since the colonization of New England was, according to his own report, gaining momentum without him. (He noted the departure in 1629 of a group of 350 colonists, the first large contingent of the Massachusetts Bay Company.) But, he insisted, his role in the colonies had been crucial. Once again he called them *his* children: "Those countries Captain Smith oft times used to call his children that never had mother, and well he might, for few fathers ever paid dearer for so little content" (893). (Smith seems even more self-pitying when he writes of himself in the third person.) Even yet, he urged, his presence in America was indispensable:

For yet those countries are not so forward but they may become as miserable as ever, if better courses be not taken than is, as this Smith will plainly demonstrate to his Majesty or any other noble person of ability, liable generously to undertake it. How within a short time to make Virginia able to resist any enemy that as yet lieth open to all, and yield the King more custom within these few years in certain staple commodities than ever it did in tobacco, which now not being worth bringing home, the custom will be as uncertain to the King as dangerous to the plantations. (894)

In 1629, when Smith wrote the above, he was still eager to return to America, though he was nearly fifty. He was somewhat less conscious, however, of his frustrations and more aware of his accomplishments; in the concluding (if penultimate) chapter of the *True Travels,* he notes that among his adventures was bringing "our New England to the subjection of the kingdom of Great Britain" (912).

IV   *Advertisements For the Unexperienced Planters*

John Smith's final work on New England was his last book: *Advertisements For the Unexperienced Planters of New England, or any where. Or The Path-way to experience to erect a Plantation* was written in October, 1630,[13] and published in 1631. From the literary point of view, it is doubtless Smith's best book. He wrote it by interrupting the composition of what would presumably have been a big book, perhaps like the *Generall Historie.* He described it as "my history of the sea" (951). Before he had finished it, he died, a great pity since he was beginning to achieve considerable literary skill.

The *Advertisements,* a forty-eight-page quarto pamphlet, pro-

Smith's newly found piety, if that is what it was, is reflected in the chapter devoted to religion in the *Advertisements*. Whereas earlier Smith had disparaged religion as a basis for colonization, or had given only cursory attention to it, he now added a new ingredient to his formula for a successful colony: the church. Smith argued that religion was an indispensable instrument of order, a preventer of factionalism: he described at some length the religious practices of the Jamestown colonists in his days in Virginia. The most important evidence that religion was now of considerable importance to Smith and helped him to develop a more philosophic attitude towards his career is the striking and powerful poem which prefaces the *Advertisements*. Presumably it is Smith's, and it surely sets forth in the first two stanzas an attitude which was very much his:

The Sea Mark[15]

Aloof, aloof, and come no near;
    the dangers do appear;
Which if my ruin had not been
    you had not seen:
I only lie upon this shelf
    to be a mark to all
    which on the same might fall,
That none may perish but myself.

If in or outward you be bound,
    do not forget to sound.
Neglect of that was cause of this,
    to steer amiss.
The seas were calm, the wind was fair,
    that made me so secure
    that now I must endure
All weathers be they foul or fair

After thus indulging in self-pity, in the last stanza Smith finds consolation.

The winter's cold, the summer's heat
    alternatively beat
Upon my bruised sides that rue
    because too true
That no relief can ever come.
But why should I despair,
    being promised so fair
That there shall be a Day of Doom. (922)

The defeated adventurer rested, assured that his achievements were responsible for the colonization of the New World and that recognition would come in time, though not in his lifetime.

In the *Advertisements* Smith continued his disparagement of the Separatists of the Plymouth Colony; he particularly disliked "their pride and singularity and contempt of authority. Because they could not be equals, they would have no superiors" (946). He seems to have been oblivious that Winthrop and the men of Massachusetts Bay were Puritans, for he reports that Winthrop and his council have been put "to their utmost wits" by some who "could not endure the name of a bishop, others not the sight of a cross nor surplice, others by no means the Book of Common Prayer" (954). These had all returned to England or moved to Plymouth, according to his story.

The book has many expressions of admiration and advice for the Massachusetts settlers. Smith argued the importance of making America a land of opportunity for all, a place where a servant might become as prosperous as his master had been in the Old Country.[16] He advised strongly against excessive taxation: "have a care that all your countrymen [that] shall come to trade with you be not troubled with pilotage, buoyage, anchorage, wharfage, custom, or any such tricks as hath been lately used in most of new plantations, where they [the leaders] would be kings before their folly, to the discouragement of many ... (961).

The contents of the *Advertisements* are, however, too varied for it to be labeled what Smith at one point called it, "a memorandum of my love" to Governor Winthrop and the other leaders of the Bay Colony "to make your plantations so near [contiguous?] and great as you can" (947).[17] Rather the theme of the book is once again the desirability of colonization and the best methods for carrying it on, with New England, not Virginia, receiving Smith's special attention. The autobiographical ramblings do not this time give the impression of having been inserted from egotism or to pad out a thin book; for they are all related to Smith's theme. Each of the fifteen chapters has some unity, and the middle chapters tell in something like chronological order the story of the exploration and settlement of New England.

The new, less defensive John Smith is most apparent in the three chapters—XII, XIII, and XV—in which he hands on to colonists and would-be colonists practical advice on farming, building forts, preparing for military combat, putting the Indians to work, and selecting good leaders. Here he does not protest too much.

Smith had mellowed and was now in much better control of himself and of the materials he wished to organize into a book. At times, he demonstrated a wonderfully disciplined sense of irony—not just in a sentence or two but in whole paragraphs. He treats in this tone what had been particularly annoying to him: the demands made on him as president of the governing council in Virginia by the controlling officials in London. He had responded by seeing to it that each ship returning to England was freighted with "only some small quantities of wainscot, clapboard, pitch, tar, rosin, soap-ashes, glass, cedar, black walnut, knees for ships, ash for pikes, iron ore none better, some silver ore but so poor it was not regarded—better there may be, for I was no mineralist—some sturgeon, but it was too tart of the vinegar (which was of my own store, for little came from them which was good), and wine of the country's wild grapes, but it was too sour, yet better than they sent us any—in two years but one hogshead of claret."

In the meantime, Smith was "only spending my time to revenge my imprisonment upon the harmless innocent savages, who by my cruelty I forced to feed me with their contribution and to send any [who] offended my idle humor to Jamestown to punish at my own discretion." These actions, the London officials claimed, were "things clean contrary to my commission, whilst I and my company took our needless pleasures in discovering the countries about us, building of forts and such unnecessary fooleries, where an egg shell (as they writ) had been sufficient against such enemies" (927–28).

Smith's account of what he had shipped to England involves considerable exaggeration, but it is much more attractive than the often embarrassingly egotistical versions Smith had told before, as in the *Generall Historie.* Even the annoying habit of borrowing from his earlier writings to make new ones is restrained in the *Advertisements.* Smith borrowed only three paragraphs from his *Description of New England* and a few briefer passages from the *True Travels.* The former, also used in the *Generall Historie,* was well worth borrowing; for it is one of the brightest passages in Smith's writings. If Smith had written more prose as controlled, he would have a much larger claim to fame:

... seeing we are not born for ourselves but each to help other, and our abilities are much alike at the hour of our birth and minute of our death; seeing our good deeds or bad, by faith in Christ's merit, is all we have to carry our souls to heaven or hell; seeing honor is our lives' ambition, and our ambition after death to have an honorable memory of our life; and seeing by no means we would be abated of the dignity and glory of our predecessors, let us imitate their virtues to be worthily their successors; or at least not hinder, if not further, them that would do their utmost and best endeavor. (935–36)

Since none of Smith's three New England publications has much structure or unity, and since each is uneven, most readers may be content with selections from the three, though the whole of the *Advertisements* is worth reading. Considerable advances in Smith's literary art are evident to one who reads the three in the order of composition (the first edition of *New Englands Trials* might be omitted), for time and perspective permitted him to achieve wisdom and philosophic resignation without losing his excitedly optimistic vision of America, especially New England. Smith's final achievement, and as a writer his greatest, was the expression of his principles and practice in powerful language. In the last chapter of the *Advertisements,* his appreciation of the virtues which he believed he had demonstrated (when given the opportunity) is not obstructed by any petty-minded bitterness.

And truly there is no pleasure comparable to a generous spirit, as good employment in noble actions, especially amongst Turks, heathen, and infidels: to see daily new countries, people, fashions, governments, strategems; relieve the oppressed, comfort his friends, pass miseries, subdue enemies, adventure upon any feasible danger for God and his country. It is true, it is a happy thing to be born to strength, wealth, and honor, but that which is got by prowess and magnanimity is the truest lustre, and those can the best distinguish content that have escaped most honorable dangers, as if, out of every extremity, he found himself now born to a new life, to learn how to amend and maintain his age. (962–63)

The words are still stirring, especially when one remembers that Smith, a self-made man, made for himself a permanent place in history in a day when men could not easily rise from the station 'of their birth. If Smith had to exaggerate his own accomplishments to write prose such as this, the deception was well worth while.

CHAPTER 9

Smith: An Assessment

A S A WRITER Captain John Smith had as his paramount concern immediate results. He was eager to return to America; he wrote in order to persuade Englishmen to send him there. He hoped that his plans to combine fishing voyages and colonization would have immediate consequences. He described Virginia because published accounts were second-hand and inaccurate; he addressed his contemporaries, for whom he wanted to set the record straight. Why he published an autobiography is not clear, but he probably did so to make money. He wrote his two books of sea terms for the same reason. Even his big book, which was in theory "for the general good of all them who belong to those plantations [in America] and all their posterity," (cxxvi), proved to be to a considerable extent not only an argument that a tough Indian policy ought to be adopted immediately but also a defense of Smith against his detractors. Yet Smith's works have lived as have few non-belletristic writings of his time. There is something of permanent interest about his subjects, his approaches, and the man himself. Perhaps an explanation can be found. It is worth trying, at any rate.

I The Man Smith

First of all, there is the man. All of his efforts to impress backers with himself and his ideas, to serve as his own press agent, were unsuccessful in his own time; but, because of them, he lives on. His portrait, published in *A Description of New England,* the account of his Virginia activities by his friends in *A Map of Virginia,* the editorializing which mars the *Historie,* and the mature philosophizing of the *Advertisements*—all contribute to make Smith a recognizable human being in a way that few of his contemporaries are.

Smith told the story of his life mostly in bits and snatches, by digressions, by efforts to correct impressions and facts, by autobiography disguised as Virginia history or as New England propaganda. Only once, in the *True Travels,* did he set out to tell his own story; and then, ironically, he devoted much of his book to borrowed accounts of the lands he had visited. Nearly always Smith described his actions, not his feelings; and he set forth his thoughts only when he supposed that his ideas might lead to action.

One sees him as an active person, encountering Turks in single combat, killing the bashaw of Nalbrits to escape captivity, exploring the northern edges of Chesapeake Bay, impressing Powhatan with his skills and his bravery, frightening the Indians into providing food for his men, mapping the New England coast, escaping from French pirates in a stormy night. He was tough, demanding, but always fair. Though frequently a leader of men, Smith seems nevertheless to have been a loner. He liked independence: he left behind the ties of home and family, and he never married.

The image of himself that Smith created was largely a legitimate one, for research has shown that he either did or probably did what he declared himself to have done. Specifically, he preserved the Virginia colony from collapse and gave a crucial impetus to interest in New England. But this self-reliant hero eventually painted a picture of himself that is decidedly overdrawn. It was a trifle pretentious of Smith to assert that he was "Admiral of New England" more than fifteen years after his one visit there, even though, according to his statement, he had been given the title for life. It was preposterous for Smith to assert in 1626 that most of the American colonies sprang from the fruits of his adventures and discoveries, or to argue in 1629 that he had brought New England to the subjection of Great Britain. These statements are perhaps not lies, but they are surely exaggerations. To suppose, however, that such boasts demonstrate Smith's inability to appreciate the truth is not accurate. The fact seems to be that Smith could only accept his frustration at being unable to return to America by supposing that whatever was happening there was the consequence of his earlier, truly significant activities.

Smith was a practical man. He should return to America merely because of his previous accomplishments. He had specific proposals, carefully drawn up. He planned to make the Virginia and New England Indians work on behalf of the colonists, as the Spaniards had done; he wanted to establish colonies to work with the fishermen who visited the New England coast each year. Both plans were practical; and, if the former seems cruel, it was less so than the alternative adopted by the Virginia colonists, the elimination of the Indians by massacre. In his last work, the *Advertisements*, Smith threw out many practical suggestions for colonists and would-be colonists. And still he sought to return to America, even at fifty, to put his ideas to work. The New Englanders will be ignorant, wrote Smith in 1630, if they do not

... in a short time cause the savages to do them as good service as their own men, as I did in Virginia, and neither use cruelty nor tyranny amongst them, a consequence well worth putting in practice, and till it be effected, they will hardly do well. I know ignorance will say it is impossible, but this impossible task ever since the massacre in Virginia I have been a suitor to have undertaken but with 150 men: to have got corn, fortified the country, and discovered them more land than they all yet know or have demonstrated. (955)

Smith was also a dreamer. He imagined a prosperous America, a place where a man could enjoy nature and its fruits. He urged cooperation in establishing colonies, but he saw no need for community. He was an individualist, and he wanted other men to have a chance to be as much. He urged men to imitate the "brave spirits that advanced themselves from poor soldiers to great captains, their posterity to great lords, and their king to be one of the greatest potentates on earth, and the fruits of their labors his greatest glory, power, and renown" (965). He admired those men, such as Columbus, Cortez, Pizarro, and Magellan, who had shown themselves wise, discreet, generous, and courageous—his four favorite virtues. He admired as did Milton, the desire for fame, " ... the spur that the clear spirit doth raise/(The last infirmity of noble mind)/To scorn delights, and live laborious days."

Above all, Smith was an American. One hundred and fifty years after Smith's death, St. Jean de Crèvecoeur was to ask, "What then is the American, this new man?" His answer might well have been Smith's: "The American," continued Crèvecoeur, "is a new man, who acts upon new principles; he must therefore entertain new ideas, and form new opinions. From involuntary idleness, servile dependence, penury, and useless labor, he has passed to toils of a very different nature, rewarded by ample subsistence.—This is an American."[1] John Smith was such a new man—or rather would have been, had he had his way. Smith is the most vivid personality of American literature before Benjamin Franklin.

II Smith the Writer

Captain John Smith was more than a vivid personality, a historical figure of unquestionable importance, and a propaganda writer who attracted attention to New England. He was also the author of works of permanent interest for the picture they provide of America on the eve of colonization—"The Description of Virginia" and *A Description of New England*—and for the story that they tell of the Jamestown colonists' struggles— *A True Relation* and Book III of the *Generall Historie.*

Smith's most attractive works are the second and third books of the *Generall Historie,* the former, "A Description of Virginia," polished into shape by an editor; the latter, Smith's revision and amplification of the work of other men. These two works, however composed, are masterful accounts of *the* place and *the* time: the land where England's first permanent American colony was established, and the first crucial two and a half years of the colony's life. In Smith's "Description," as Moses Coit Tyler has observed, "all the dull and hard details of the subject [are] made delightful by felicities of phrase that seem to spring up as easily as wild flowers in the woods of his own Virginia."[2] The book is truly both *dulce* and *utile*—sweet and useful. If Smith's contributions in Book III are not of the sort that entitles him to be considered a historian, nevertheless they do make a very good book even better.

The art of Book III has been ignored in the controversy over the Pocahontas story. Howard Mumford Jones called the earlier version, the "Proceedings," an epic account.[3] The work of many writers, the "Proceedings" with Smith's additions is even better. Book III is characterized by richness and literary integrity, and it is full of incident and character. Its fate at the hands of historians of literature has been most unfortunate. If Smith does not deserve all the credit for the final product, this fact should not continue to prevent the work itself from being recognized as a masterful narrative.

The "Proceedings" was inaccurately referred to in the *Cambridge History of American Literature* as "supplemental chapters on events in the colony from June, 1608, to the end of 1609."[4] (In fact it begins in December, 1606, and stops around September, 1609). Next to nothing is said about Book III, except for comments on Smith's rescue by Pocahontas. The more recent *Literary History of the United States* ignored the "Proceedings" in both bibliography and text, where of Book III of the *Historie* it is again only the Pocahontas story that receives attention. "Consider the Pocahontas story—and one cannot well avoid it. Smith's own account in 1608 is matter-of-fact. When he retold it in 1624, the story had been gorgeously and glamorously enlarged."[5] In fact, there is no "Pocahontas story" in the 1608 account; and the rescue by Pocahontas occupies less than a sentence in Smith's 1624 account of his captivity. (See Chapter 6.)

True enough, Smith had a personal point to make in preparing

Book III; but it did not relate to Pocahontas. He used the *Historie* to further his campaign to return to America. But, since he was a writer only by force of circumstances, he ought to be forgiven such subjectivity by critics who might be grateful to Smith for making available to a wide audience the best contemporary account of the beginning of the Virginia colony with valuable additions of his own. *A True Relation*, Smith's earlier account, is rather less good; for it was written in great haste and was not intended for publication. Yet it has undeniable merits and is sometimes more detailed and graphic, as the following passages should demonstrate.

"Proceedings" and Book III

The next day Newport came ashore and received as much content as these people could give him. A boy named Thomas Savage was then given unto Powhatan, whom Newport called his son, for whom Powhatan gave him Namontack, his trusty servant and one of a shrewd, subtle capacity. (102, 405)

A True Relation
But seeing Captain Newport and Master Scrivener coming ashore, the King returned to his home and I went to meet him [Newport]. With a trumpet before him, we marched to the king, who after his old manner kindly received him, especially a boy of thirteen years old, called Thomas Savage, whom he [Newport] gave him as his son. He requited this kindness with each of us a great basket of beans. And entertaining him with the former discourse, we passed away that day and agreed to bargain the next day, and so returned to the pinnace. (27)

The fuller account of the *True Relation* is somewhat obscure, especially in its pronoun references; and it does not report the gift of Namontack, who was later important in the colonists' relations with the Indians. But the picture it provides is much more vivid.

The *Generall Historie* is difficult to evaluate as a whole. The fact that is a large, unusually handsome book, not a thin pamphlet, has given it special importance. As a compilation, it has been long admired and read, especially by historically minded Virginians, of whom there were and are many. But, except for the second and third books and a portion of the sixth, it has no special authority; and, unlike Bradford's *Of Plymouth Plantation*, it is not susceptible to being trimmed and modernized for modern readers. Selections such as those recently prepared by John Lankford in *Captain John Smith's America* should, however, make the *Historie* more accessible.

A Description of New England, republished as a portion of Book

VI of the *Generall Historie,* is also important among Smith's writings. Without the sense of form of Books II and III, it still has much to recommend it, especially a spirit of excitement about the discoveries that Smith had made and the plans they had inspired. Much better, however, is Smith's last pamphlet, *Advertisements For the unexperienced Planters.* It too lacks an adequate organizing principle, but it is not so shapeless as the *Description.* Its special virtue is the quality of its prose.

The prose of Smith's England is among the great glories of literature. In the *Advertisements* Smith gave America some of this inheritance, though his prose, as in this passage from the preface, is perhaps better described as Elizabethan in its vigor and in its exuberant irregularity:

Appelles by the proportion of a foot could make the whole proportion of a man. Were he now living, he might go to school, for now are thousands can, by opinion, proportion kingdoms, cities, and lordships, that never durst adventure to see them. Malignancy I expect from those [that] have lived ten or twelve years in those action and return as wise as they went, claiming time and experience for their tutor, that can neither shift sun nor moon,[6] nor say their compass, yet will tell you of more than all the world, betwixt the Exchange, Paul's [St. Paul's Cathedral], and Westminster. So it be news, it matters not what: that will pass current when truth must be stayed with an army of conceits that can make a man anything, and tell as well what all England is seeing but Milford Haven, as what Apelles was by the picture of his great toe. (921)

The most admirable quality of Smith's style is its concreteness. Smith's concern for fact, his acute awareness of the world around him as he moved into unknown lands, gave him great assistance when he turned to writing. Time and again, sometimes unexpectedly, one finds in Smith's prose precise pictures of what he saw in the New World. Here, for example, is his description of the first churches in Virginia:

When I first went to Virginia [he wrote, twenty-three years later] I well remember we did hang an awning (which is an old sail) to three or four trees to shadow us from the sun. Our walls were rails of wood, our seats unhewed trees till we cut planks, our pulpit a bar of wood nailed to two neighboring trees. In foul weather we shifted into an old rotten tent, for we had few better. . . . This was our church, till we built a homely thing like a barn, set upon cratchets, covered with rafts, sedge, and earth, so was also the walls. (957)

Smith's acute perceptiveness sometimes reveals itself in a sentence or a phrase, as in his observation on the trees of the New England coast: "Oak is the chief wood, of which there is a great difference in regard to the soil where it groweth" (207).

Captain John Smith is, then, for many reasons a writer of singular importance in the early period of American literature. He was America's first writer, one of whom Americans can be proud. He was

> On fire, yes, fed or fasting, to see new things,
> Explore, map out, taste, venture, enjoy, astound,
> And look, look, look, with a fly's remembering eye. . . . [7]

Notes and References

Preface

1. Stephen Vincent Benét, *Western Star* (New York, 1943), p. 72.
2. B. Smith, *Captain John Smith* (Philadelphia, 1953), p. 307.

Chapter One

1. Irving Story, "Elizabethan Prelude," *Pacific University Studies in Literature,* #3 (November, 1942), p. 11.
2. James A. Williamson, *Sir Francis Drake* (Hamden, Conn., 1966), pp. 9–72; S. T. Bindoff, *Tudor England* (Harmsworth, 1950), pp. 247–62.
3. James A. Williamson, *The Tudor Age* (New York, 1964), pp. 53–58, 70–71; Charles M. Andrews, *The Colonial Period in American History* (New Haven, 1933), I, 16–17. The extent of the Cabot voyages is now considered very uncertain.
4. James A. Williamson, *The Age of Drake* (London, 1938), pp. 224–34, and Edward Haie, "A Report of the voyage and successe therof, attempted in the year of our Lord 1583 by sir Humfrey Gilbert knight," in Richard Hakluyt, *The Principal Voyages* (Glasgow, 1904), VIII, 34–77.
5. See George B. Parks, *Richard Hakluyt and the English Voyages* (New York, 1928), on which much of the following account of Hakluyt is based. See also John Parker, *Books to Build an Empire* (Amsterdam, 1965).
6. The work is included in E. G. R. Taylor, ed., *The Original Writings and Correspondence of the Two Richard Hakluyts* (Hakluyt Soc., 1935).
7. See David B. Quinn, *Raleigh and the British Empire* (London, 1962), pp. 58 ff.
8. Wallace Notestein, *The English People on the Eve of Colonization, 1603–1630* (New York, 1962), p. 255. Boies Penrose is among the many to refer to Hakluyt's work as the great prose epic of the Elizabethan period. See Penrose, *Travel and Discovery in the Renaissance, 1420–1620* (Cambridge, 1952), p. 318.
9. A. L. Rowse, *The Expansion of Elizabethan England* (New York, 1955), p. 209.
10. Louis B. Wright, *The Colonial Search for a Southern Eden* (University, Alabama, 1953), pp. 7 ff.
11. Andrews, *Colonial Period*, I, 20–21, and E. G. R. Taylor, *Late Tudor and Early Stuart Geography, 1583–1650* (London, 1934), p. 2.
12. Taylor, *Geography*, pp. 2–3.
13. James A. Williamson, *The Ocean in English History* (Oxford, 1941), p. 67.
14. See Louis B. Wright, *Middle-Class Culture in Elizabethan England* (Ithaca, 1958), pp. 508–35.
15. The best edition is that of David B. Quinn, *The Roanoke Voyages,*

1584–1590 (Hakluyt Soc., 1955), pp. 317–77.

16. Quinn, *Roanoke Voyages*, p. 37.

17. The drawings are reproduced in Stefan Lorant, *The New World. The First Pictures of America* (New York, 1946).

18. A. L. Rowse, *The Elizabethans and America* (New York, 1965), p. 189.

19. See Quinn, *Roanoke Voyages*, p. 389 (note).

20. It is to be found in Quinn, *Roanoke Voyages*, pp. 255–94.

21. See V. T. Harlow's edition of Raleigh's *Discoverie of the large and bewtiful Empire of Guiana* (London, 1948), pp. l–li.

22. Raleigh, *Guiana*, p. 73.

23. See Ernest A. Strathmann, *Sir Walter Raleigh: A Study in Elizabethan Skepticism* (New York, 1951).

24. Nicholas Monardes wrote *Joyfull Newes out of the Newfounde Worlde*, an account of American commodities; it was published in English in 1577.

25. C. S. Lewis, *English Literature in the Sixteenth Century* (Oxford, 1954), p. 437.

26. For information about Brereton and the voyage, see Warner F. Gookin and Philip L. Barbour, *Bartholomew Gosnold* (Hamden, Conn., 1963). I use the facsimile reprint of Brereton published in New York in 1903.

27. I use the edition in Henry S. Burrage, ed., *Early English and American Voyages*, Original Narratives Series (New York, 1932), which also includes Brereton's *Relation*.

28. Andrews, *Colonial Period*, I, 78–97.

29. I use the edition of Louis B. Wright entitled *A Voyage to Virginia in 1609* (Charlottesville, 1964).

30. See *The Complete Works of Shakespeare*, ed. George L. Kittredge (Boston, 1936), pp. 3–4; *The Tempest*, ed. Louis B. Wright and Virginia La Mar (New York, 1961), pp. ix–xi; and Rowse, *The Elizabethans and America*, pp. 197–200.

31. Moses Coit Tyler, *A History of American Literature, 1607–1765* (New York, 1962), p. 65.

32. See Alexander Whitaker, *Good Newes From Virginia* (London, 1613), with preface by William Crashaw; and also Lewis Hughes, "A Letter Sent into England from the Summer Islands" (1615) in Louis B. Wright, *The Elizabethans' America* (Cambridge, 1965), pp. 202–205.

33. I use the edition of Louis B. Wright and Virginia Freund (Hakluyt Soc., 1953).

34. Parks, *Richard Hakluyt*, pp. 203–206, 219–22.

35. Taylor, *Geography*, p. 53.

36. Parks, *Hakluyt*, pp. 183–93, 223–25. Parks notes that the four volumes of the *Pilgrimes* contain 3,900,000 words, of which a little more than 40% is material collected by Hakluyt, some having appeared in his *Voyages*. A good account of Purchas is to be found in Louis B. Wright, *Religion and Empire* (Chapel Hill, 1943), pp. 115–33.

37. For Coleridge's interest in Purchas, see John Livingston Lowes, *The*

Road to Xanadu (Cambridge, 1927).

38. See Philip L. Barbour, *The Three Worlds of Captain John Smith* (Boston, 1964), pp. 354–55.

39. Wright, *The Cultural Life of the American Colonies, 1607–1763* (New York, 1962), p. 156.

Chapter Two

1. B. Smith, *Captain John Smith* (Philadelphia, 1953), p. 263.

2. *Ibid.*, p. 344.

3. *Ibid.*, pp. 16–17.

4. See Mildred Campbell, *The English Yeoman under Elizabeth and the Early Stuarts* (New Haven, 1942).

5. See B. Smith, *John Smith*, pp. 17–18.

6. See Wallace Notestein, *The English People on the Eve of Colonization, 1603–1630* (New York, 1962), pp. 116–29.

7. Philip Barbour, *The Three Worlds of Captain John Smith* (Boston, 1964), pp. 11–16.

8. See the very informative discussion in Barbour, *Smith*, pp. 78 ff., to which the following account is much indebted.

9. See *Hakluytus Posthumus, or Purchas His Pilgrimes* (Glasgow, 1905–1907), VIII, 342.

10. John Smith, *Travels and Works* (Edinburgh, 1910), pp. xxxiii–xxxv.

11. The account of Smith's Virginia adventures is based on "The Proceedings of the English Colony in Virginia," the second part of *A Map of Virginia* (1612), published in Smith, *Travels and Works;* and on Barbour, *Smith.*

12. Alexander Brown, ed., *The Genesis of the United States* (Boston, 1891), p. 102.

13. Barbour, *Smith*, p. 293.

14. Well told by Barbour, pp. 317–19.

15. The remainder of this account is based chiefly on Smith's writings.

Chapter Three

1. Several are printed in the Arber-Bradley edition of Smith's *Works*, pp. xxxviii–xci.

2. Worthington C. Ford suggested that "I. H.," author of the epistle, may be John Healey, a hack writer. See Ford, "Tyndall's Map of Virginia," *Massachusetts Historical Society Proceedings*, VIII (1924–1925), 246.

3. B. Smith, *Captain John Smith*, p. 116.

4. Barbour, *The Three Worlds of Captain John Smith*, pp. 291–92.

5. The Instructions had suggested that a lake might be a passageway to the Pacific. See above, Chapter 2, section IV.

6. Or so said Smith, in the *Generall Historie.* See *Works*, p. 444, where he reported that whereas Newport had boasted that he would "leave us victuals for twelve months . . . we were constrained to give him three hogs-

heads of that [corn] to victual him homeward."

7. Howard Mumford Jones, *The Literature of Virginia in the Seventeenth Century* (Charlottesville, 1968), p. 42 (note). It is more likely that something was left out just before the last paragraph to fit the material into the printer's gatherings.

8. See, for example, Alexander Brown, *The Genesis of the United States* (Boston, 1891), p. 201 (note).

9. Tyler, *A History of American Literature, 1607–1765*, p. 52.

10. Jones, *Literature*, p. 5.

11. *Ibid.*, pp. 121–22.

12. McCary, *John Smith's Map of Virginia* (Williamsburg, 1957), p. 9.

13. Jones, *Literature*, p. 48.

14. *Ibid.*, p. 49.

15. William Randel, "Captain John Smith's Attitude Towards the Indians," *Virginia Magazine of History and Biography*, XLVII (1939), 218–29.

16. See above, pp. 37–8.

17. Keith Glenn, "Captain John Smith and the Indians," *Virginia Magazine of History and Biography*, LII (1944), 228–48.

18. Roy Harvey Pearce, *The Savages of North America*, revised edition (Baltimore, 1965), p. 14.

19. Perry Miller, *Errand into the Wilderness* (New York, 1964), pp. 101–106.

20. Ben McCary, *Indians in Seventeenth-Century Virginia* (Williamsburg, 1957), pp. 62–65. See also Regina Flannery, *Analysis of Coastal Algonquian Culture* (Washington, 1939), p. 94.

21. Maurice A. Mook suggested that Smith was interested in ethnology for its own sake. See Mook, "Virginia Ethnology from an Early Relation," *William and Mary Quarterly*, 2nd series, XXIII (1943), 103.

Chapter Four

1. Richard S. Dunn, "Seventeenth-Century English Historians of America," in *Seventeenth-Century America*, ed. James Morton Smith (Chapel Hill, 1959).

2. Jarvis M. Morse, *American Beginnings* (Washington, 1952), p. 3.

3. Edwin C. Rozwenc, "Captain John Smith's Image of America," *William and Mary Quarterly*, 3rd series, XVI (1959), 28, 36.

4. Brown, *The Genesis of the United States*, p. 1010.

5. Susan Kingsbury, ed., *The Records of the Virginia Company of London* (Washington, 1906–1935), I, 451.

6. For Smith's summary of the company's reaction, see the *Historie*, pp. 590–91.

7. B. Smith, *Captain John Smith*, p. 263.

8. See the edition of Strachey's work edited by Louis B. Wright and Virginia Freund (Hakluyt Soc., 1953).

9. Smith himself provided this information; see *Works*, p. 331.

10. The prospectus was published in facsimile form by Luther S. Living-

ston as *Captain John Smith's Circular or Prospectus* (Cambridge, 1914).

11. For Sandys and Fotherby, see Philip L. Barbour, "Captain John Smith and the Bishop of Sarum," *Huntington Library Quarterly,* XXVI (1962), 11–29.

12. R. Hakluyt, ed., *The Principal Navigations, Voyages, Traffiques, and Discoveries* (Glasgow, 1903–1905), VII, 297 ff.

13. In Hakluyt, VII, 310 ff.

14. In *Hakluytus Posthumus or Purchas His Pilgrimes* (Glasgow, 1905–1907), XVIII, 322 ff.

15. In Purchas, XVIII, 335 ff.

16. Alexander Brown, Smith's severest critic, considered the whole of the *Generall Historie* in this light in "Some Notes on Smith's *Historie,*" *New England Historical and Genealogical Register,* XLVII (1893), 205–11.

17. See E. G. Swem and John M. Jennings, *A Selected Bibliography of Virginia, 1607–1699* (Richmond, 1957).

18. J. Franklin Jameson, *The History of Historical Writing in America* (Boston, 1891), p. 6.

19. Brown, *Genesis,* p. 788 (note).

20. Ed. J. H. Lefroy (Hakluyt Soc., 1882), its first publication. Lefroy thought that Smith wrote the work because of the borrowings in the *Generall Historie.*

21. First published in *John Pory's Lost Description of Plymouth,* ed. Champlin Burrage (Boston, 1918). Smith referred to this work as "a plot of Richard Norwood" (p. 942).

22. See the edition of Dwight B. Heath, entitled *A Journal of the Pilgrims at Plymouth* (New York, 1963), from which I quote.

23. See Barbour, *Smith,* pp. 367–68.

24. *Ibid.,* p. 368.

Chapter Five

1. Morse, "Captain John Smith and His Critics," *Journal of Southern History,* I (1935), 132.

2. See above, p. 63.

3. See Philip L. Barbour, *The Three Worlds of Captain John Smith,* pp. 298, 301.

4. Smith mentioned his rescue at two other points in the *Historie:* in the letters to the Queen included in Book IV (see above, Chapter 4) and in the prefatory epistle, where he listed Pocahontas as one of the "honorable and virtuous ladies" who had come to his aid. "In the utmost of many extremities, that blessed Pocahontas, the great king's daughter of Virginia, oft saved my life" (p. 276).

5. See Keith Glenn, "Captain John Smith and the Indians," *Virginia Magazine of History and Biography,* LII (1944), 228–48.

6. Barbour, *Smith,* p. 233; Tyler, *A History of American Literature, 1607–1765,* pp. 53–55.

7. Barbour argued that since Smith was intended to have an important

post in the new government of the colony, his letter did not offend the London officials. See Barbour, *Smith*, p. 287.

8. See Wingfield's version in his "Discourse of Virginia," in the Arber-Bradley edition of Smith's *Works*, p. lxxxiii.

Chapter Six

1. Barbour, *The Three Worlds of Captain John Smith*, p. 375.
2. *Ibid.*, p. 377.
3. I am much indebted to Mr. Barbour, who kindly communicated this information to me. He is currently undertaking a comparison of the *Accidence*, the *Sea Grammar*, and the *Nomenclator Navalis;* and I trust that he will publish the results.
4. See G. E. Manwaring and W. G. Perrin, *The Life and Works of Sir Henry Mainwaring* (Navy Records Soc., 1920–1922), II, 69–73. This work includes an edition of the *Nomenclator Navalis* or *Dictionary*, based on manuscript copies.
5. Franklin B. Williams, *Index of Dedications and Commendatory Verses in English Books Before 1641* (London, 1962), p. xi.
6. These poems were published for the first time since the seventeenth century as "Two 'Unknown' Poems by Captain John Smith," ed. Philip L. Barbour, *Virginia Magazine of History and Biography*, LXXV (1967), 156–57.

Chapter Seven

1. See Deane's edition of "A Discourse of Virginia" by Edward Maria Wingfield, in American Antiquarian Society, *Archaelogica Americana*, IV (1860), 67–103; Deane, ed., *A True Relation* (Boston, 1866); Adams, "Captain John Smith," *North American Review*, CIV (1867), 1–30; Kropf, "Notes," *Notes and Queries*, 7th series, IX (1890), 1–2, 41–43, 102–104, 161–62, 223–24, 281–82.
2. Jones, *The Literature of Virginia in the Seventeenth Century*, p. 54.
3. Morse, "John Smith and His Critics: A Chapter in Colonial Historiography," *Journal of Southern History*, I (1935), 130.
4. Barbour, *The Three Worlds of Captain John Smith*, p. 394; Barbour, "Fact and Fiction in Captain John Smith's *True Travels*," in *Literature as a Mode of Travel*, ed. Warner G. Rice (1963); B. Smith, *Captain John Smith* (1953).
5. Though I cite, as usual, the Arber-Bradley edition, a very convenient modern edition of the *Travels* is that of John Gould Fletcher and Lawrence C. Wroth (New York, 1930).
6. *Hakluytus Posthumus, or Purchas His Pilgrimes* (Glasgow, 1905–1907), VIII, 325.
7. Barbour, *Smith*, p. 373.
8. Fletcher, ed., *True Travels*, p. vi.

Chapter Eight

1. Samuel Eliot Morison, *Builders of the Bay Colony* (Boston, 1958), p. 6.

2. Barbour, *The Three Worlds of Captain John Smith*, p. 325.

3. Henry F. Howe, *Prologue to New England* (New York, 1943), p. 271. My discussion of Smith's writings on New England is indebted to Howe's study.

4. No evidence apart from Smith's writings exists of his having been given the title, though it seems likely that he was.

5. E. G. R. Taylor, *Late Tudor and Early Stuart Geography, 1583–1650*, p. 167.

6. Smith was much offended that Thomas Hunt, master of one of the ships in his voyage of 1614, captured and sold into slavery twenty-seven Indians. He tells the story several times, first in the *Description*, p. 219.

7. See Sigmund Diamond, "From Organization to Society: Virginia in the Seventeenth Century," *American Journal of Sociology*, LXIII (1958), 403–404.

8. The passage continues: "If he have but the taste of virtue and magnanimity, what to such a mind can be more pleasant, than planting and building a foundation for his posterity, got from the rude earth, by God's blessing and his own industry, without prejudice to any? If he have any grain of faith or zeal in religion, what can he do less hurtful to any, or more agreeable to God, than to seek to convert those poor savages to know Christ, and humanity, whose labors with discretion will triple requite thy charge and pains? What so truly suits with honor and honesty as the discovering things unknown? erecting towns, peopling countries, informing the ignorant, reforming things unjust, teaching virtue; and gain to our native mother-country a kingdom to attend her, find employment for those that are idle, because they know not what to do—so far from wronging any as to cause posterity to remember thee, and remembering thee, ever honor that remembrance with praise?" Peter Michelson, commenting on this passage, finds it to be an early expression of characteristic American attitudes: "Here is the stuff of our America-first vocabulary—our chauvinistic celebrations of democracy, property, empire builders, moral superiority, religious mission, world reform, and the hammerhead work ethic. And the irony is that Smith himself is transfixed by his own rhetoric. What begins as an enticement for colonizers becomes moral apology, national prophecy, and religious liturgy. From the beginning, then, we have had Right, Destiny, and God on our side." See Michelson, "Pop Goes America," *The New Republic*, CLVII (September 2, 1967), 25. One may agree that Smith's attitude became characteristic without accepting the full dimension of Michelson's thesis.

9. See *Works*, p. 937, for Smith's account.

10. For an account of these and others of Smith's contributions, see George R. Stewart, *Names on the Land* (New York, 1945).

11. The letter is published in *Works,* cxxi–cxxiii.

12. Wilberforce Eames in *Bibliotheca Americana,* ed. Joseph Sabin and others (New York, 1868–1937), XX, 248–49. Smith continued his policy of seeking aid from London guilds. A copy of the first edition of the *Generall Historie* in the Huntington Library has inscribed on a flyleaf a letter "To the Worshipful the Master Wardens and Society of the Cordwainers of the City of London." There Smith sought support from the shoemakers for American colonization by noting "what vent your commodities have," "how many thousands of shoes have been transported to these plantations." Smith told also, in a pleasant personal note, how "for want of shoes among the oyster banks [in Virginia] we tore our hats and clothes, and those being worn, we tied barks of trees about our feet to keep them from being cut by the shells among which we must go or starve." See the whole letter in Louis B. Wright, ed., *The Elizabethans' America* (Cambridge, 1965), p. 278.

13. See *Works,* p. 955.

14. Rowse, *The Elizabethans and America,* p. 208.

15. A sea mark is an elevated object which serves to guide mariners.

16. John Lankford discussed Smith's social theory in *John Smith's America* (New York, 1967), pp. xxi–xxv. See also Edwin C. Rozwenc, "Captain John Smith's Image of America."

17. Lankford entitled his recent abridgment of the *Advertisements* "A Memorandum to John Winthrop and the Massachusetts Colonists." See *Captain John Smith's America,* p. 164.

Chapter Nine

1. Crèvecoeur, *Letters from an American Farmer,* letter three.

2. Tyler, *A History of American Literature, 1607–1765,* p. 56.

3. Jones, *The Literature of Virginia in the Seventeenth Century,* p. 25.

4. John Spencer Bassett, "The Historians, 1607–1783," *The Cambridge History of American Literature,* ed. W. P. Trent and others (New York, 1943; first published 1917), p. 16.

5. R. G. Adams, "Reports and Chronicles," *Literary History of the United States,* ed. R. E. Spiller and others (New York, 1948), I, 33.

6. Record their positions.

7. Stephen Vincent Benét, *Western Star,* p. 72.

Selected Bibliography

PRIMARY SOURCES

Although many editions of Smith's individual works exist, most readers will prefer to consult the standard collected edition, *Travels and Works of Captain John Smith*, edited by Edward Arber. A New Edition with a Biographical and Critical Introduction by A. G. Bradley. Two volumes. Edinburgh: John Grant, 1910. This edition was reprinted in 1966 by Burt Franklin, New York, and I have used it. Practically identical, except for Bradley's introduction and a sketchy bibliography by Thomas Seccombe, is Arber's edition in The English Scholar's Library, Birmingham, 1884, and Westminster, 1895.

Arber's edition omits *A Sea Grammar* (1627); the augmented version of *An Accidence* (1626); the prospectus to the *Generall Historie;* the letter to the Cordwainers, and the two commendatory verses. The *Grammar* may be found conveniently in *The Generall Historie...Together with The True Travels, Adventures, and Observations, and A Sea Grammar.* Two volumes. Glasgow: James MacLehose and Sons, 1907. I have used this edition. It is much to be hoped that Philip L. Barbour will be able to publish a new edition of Smith's works, as he now plans to do.

Below are listed Smith's works in chronological order. It has not seemed useful to cite publishers for works published before 1800. I list a few modern editions of importance.

A True Relation of such occurences and accidents of noate as hath hapned in Virginia since the first planting of that Collony, which is now resident in the South part thereof, till the last returne from there. London, 1608. In *Narratives of Early Virginia, 1606–1625,* ed. Lyon Gardiner Tyler. Original Narratives of Early American History. New York: Charles Scribner's Sons, 1907. And, with valuable notes, in *The Jamestown Voyages Under the First Charter 1606–1609,* ed. Philip L. Barbour. The Hakluyt Society. Cambridge: At the University Press, 1969.

"A Description of Virginia," in *A Map of Virginia. With a Description of that Countrey, the Commodities, People, Government and Religion.* Oxford, 1612. Also in *Narratives of Early Virginia,* as above, and with useful introduction and notes, in Hakluyt Society edition of *The Jamestown Voyages,* ed. Philip Barbour.

A Description of New England: Or the Observations and discoveries, of Captain John Smith (Admirall of that Country) in the North of America, in the year of our Lord 1614: with the successe of sixe Ships, that went the next yeare 1615; and the accidents befell him among the French men of warre: With the proofe of the present benefit this Countrey affoords: whither this present yeare, 1616, eight voluntary Ships are gone to make further tryall. London, 1616.

New Englands Trials. Declaring the successe of 26 Ships employed thither within these six yeares: with the benefit of that Countrey by sea and land: and how to build three-score sayle of good Ships, to make a little Navie Royall. London, 1620.

New Englands Trials. Declaring the successe of 80 Ships employed thither within these eight yeares; and the benefit of that Countrey by Sea and Land. With the present estate of that happie Plantation, begun but by 60 weake men in the yeare 1620. And how to build a Fleete of good Shippes to make a little Navie Royall. The second Edition. London, 1622.

The generall History of Virginia, the Somer Iles, and New England, with the names of the adventurers, and their adventures. [London, 1623.] An advance circular for the *Historie.* Reprinted as *Captain John Smith's Circular or Prospectus of His Generall Historie of Virginia, New-England, and the Summer Isles.* With notes [by Luther S. Livingston]. Cambridge: Privately Printed. 1924.

The Generall Historie of Virginia, New England, and the Summer Isles: with the names of the Adventurers, Planters, and Governours from their first beginning. Ano: 1584, to this present 1624. With the Proceedings of those Severall Colonies and the Accidents that befell them in all their Journyes and Discoveries. Also the Maps and Descriptions of all those Countryes, their Commodities, people, Government, Customes, and Religion yet knowne. Divided into sixe Bookes. London, 1624. Facsimile reprint. Cleveland: World Publishing Company, 1966. Historical introduction by A. L. Rowse; bibliographical notes by Robert O. Dougen. Another facsimile: Ann Arbor: University Microfilms, 1967.

"To The Worshipfull the Master Wardens & Societie of the Cordwayners of ye Cittie of London." A letter in the Huntington Library copy of the *Generall Historie,* published in Smith bibliography, *Bibliotheca Americana,* ed. Joseph Sabin and others. New York, Bibliographical Society of America, 1869–1937. XX, 238. Also in *The Elizabethans' America.* Ed. Louis B. Wright. Cambridge: Harvard University Press, 1965.

An Accidence or The Path-way to Experience. Necessary for all Young Sea-men, or those that are desirous to goe to Sea, briefly shewing the Phrases, Offices, and Words of Command, Belonging to the Building, Ridging, and Sayling, a Man of Warre; And how to manage a Fight at Sea. Together with the Charge and Duty of every Officer, and their Shares: Also the Names, Weight, Charge, Shot, and Powder, of all sorts of great Ordnance. With the use of the Petty Tally. London, 1626.

A Sea Grammar, With The Plaine Exposition of Smiths Accidence for young Sea-men, enlarged. Divided into fifteene Chapters: what they are you may partly conceive by the Contents. London, 1627. Subsequent editions 1653, 1691, 1692, 1699, entitled *The Sea-mans Grammar.*

"John Smith of his friend Master John Taylor and his Armado." In John Taylor, *An Armado.* London, 1627. Also in "Two 'Unknown' Poems by

Captain John Smith," ed. Philip L. Barbour, *Virginia Magazine of History and Biography*, LXXV (1967), 157–58.

"In the due Honor of the Author Master Robert Norton, and his Worke." In Robert Norton, *The Gunner*. London, 1628. Also in "Two 'Unknown' Poems," as above.

The True Travels, Adventures, and Observations of Captaine Iohn Smith, In Europe, Asia, Affrica, and America, from Anno Domini 1593. to 1629. His Accidents and Sea-fights in the Straights; his Service and Stategems of warre in Hungaria, Transilvania, Wallachia, and Moldavia, against the Turks, and Tartars; his three single combats betwixt the Christian Armie and the Turkes. After how he was taken prisoner by the Turks, sold for a Slave, sent into Tartaria; his description of the Tartars, their strange manners and customes of Religions, Diets, Buildings, Warres, Feasts, Ceremonies, and Living; how hee slew the Bashaw of Nalbrits in Cambia, and escaped from the Turkes and Tartars. Together with a continuation of his generall History of Virginia, Summer-Iles, New England, and their proceedings, since 1624. to this present 1629; as also of the new Plantations of the great River of the Amazons, the Iles of St. Christopher, Mevis, and Barbados in the West Indies. All written by actuall Authours, whose names you shall finde along the History. London, 1630. With an introduction by John Gould Fletcher and bibliographical notes by Lawrence C. Wroth. New York: Rimington & Hooper, 1930.

Advertisements For the unexperienced Planters of New England, or any where. Or, The Path-way to experience to erect a Plantation. With the yearely proceedings of this Country in Fishing and planting, since the yeare 1614. to the yeare 1630. and their present estate. Also how to prevent the greatest inconveniences, by their proceedings in Virginia, and other Plantations, by approved example. With the Countries Armes, a description of the Coast, Harbours, Habitations, Land-markes, Latitude and Longitude: with the Map, allowed by our Royall King Charles. London, 1631. Somewhat abridged in *Captain John Smith's America: Selections From His Writings*, ed. John Lankford. New York: Harper & Row, 1967.

SECONDARY SOURCES

A. *About Smith*

ADAMS, RANDOLPH G. "Notes on the Engraved Portraits of Captain John Smith," *William and Mary Quarterly*, 2nd series, XXI (1941), 27–28. Discusses changes in Smith's portrait printed on map of New England.

ANDREWS, MATTHEW PAGE. *The Soul of a Nation: The Founding of Virginia and the Projection of New England.* New York: Charles Scribner's Sons, 1943. Full discussion of Smith's work in Virginia; rambling but interesting.

BARBOUR, PHILIP L. "Captain John Smith and the Bishop of Sarum," *Huntington Library Quarterly*, XXVI (1962), 11–29. Discusses Smith's borrowings from Bishop Fotherby's *Atheomastix* (1622) in the *Generall Historie*.

———. "Captain John Smith's Observations on Life in Tartary," *Virginia Magazine of History and Biography*, LXVIII (1960), 271–83. Notes Smith's borrowings in the *True Travels*.

———. "Captain John Smith's Route through Turkey and Russia," *William and Mary Quarterly*, 3rd series, XIV (1957), 358–69. Demonstrates reliability of Smith's version of the trip in the *True Travels*.

———. "Fact and Fiction in Captain John Smith's *True Travels.*" *Literature as a Mode of Travel*. Introduction by Warner G. Rice. New York: The New York Public Library, 1963. A valuable article that seeks to show Smith's reliability. Much of the same material is to be found in Barbour's *Three Worlds of Captain John Smith*.

———. "A French Account of Captain John Smith's Adventures in the Azores, 1615," *Virginia Magazine of History and Biography*, LXXII (1964), 293–303. Shows that French records substantiate Smith's account of his adventures.

———. "A Note on the Discovery of the Original Will of Captain John Smith: With a Verbatim Transcription," *William and Mary Quarterly*, 3rd Series, XXV (1968), 625–28.

———. *Pocahontas and Her World*, Boston: Houghton Mifflin Company. 1970. A valuable discussion of Pocahontas's relationship to Smith, the Virginia Indians, and related matters.

———. *The Three Worlds of Captain John Smith*, Boston: Houghton Mifflin Company, 1964. Authoritative biography. Includes a very full bibliography.

———. "Toponymy in the Service of Biography," *Names*, XXI (1964), 108–18. On Smith's use of names on his maps.

BLACKSTONE, WALTER. "Captain John Smith: His Role in American Colonial History," in *Florida State University Studies*, #6, 1952, 23–45.

BROWN, ALEXANDER. "Some notes on Smith's History," *New England Historical and Genealogical Register*, XLVII (1893), 205–11. Very thorough attack on Smith as a special pleader in the *Generall Historie*.

CHATTERTON, E. KEBLE. *Captain John Smith*. Golden Hind Series. New York: Harper and Brothers, 1927. A well written life, outdated by Bradford Smith's and Barbour's.

DUNN, RICHARD S. "Seventeenth-Century English Historians of America." *Seventeenth-Century America*. Ed. James Morton Smith. Chapel Hill: University of North Carolina Press, 1959. Good account of Smith as a historian.

EAMES, WILBERFORCE. Bibliography of Captain John Smith. In Joseph Sabin and others, *Bibliotheca Americana: A Dictionary of Books Relating to America*. 29 volumes. New York: Bibliographical Society of America, 1868–1937. XX, 218–63. Reprinted separately. New York:

Bibliographical Society of America, 1927. Extremely valuable.

FISHWICK, MARSHALL. "Was Captain John Smith a Liar?" *American Heritage*, IX (October, 1958), 29–33, 110–11. One of the many histories of Smith's reputation.

FLETCHER, JOHN GOULD. *John Smith—Also Pocahontas.* New York: Brentano's, 1928. Light and insubstantial, but considered the best biography before Bradford Smith's.

GLENN, KEITH. "Captain John Smith and the Indians," *Virginia Magazine of History and Biography*, LII (1944), 228–48. Intelligent discussion; more acute than that of Randel (below).

GUMMERE, RICHARD M. *The American Colonial Mind and the Classical Tradition.* Cambridge: Harvard University Press, 1963. Includes a half-dozen pages on Smith's classical interests but reaches no profound conclusions.

HENRY, WILLIAM WIRT. "The Settlement at Jamestown," *Proceedings of the Virginia Historical Society* (1882), pp. 10–63. An able defense of Smith.

HUBBELL, JAY B. "The Smith-Pocahontas Story in Literature," *Virginia Magazine of History and Biography*, LXV (1957), 275–300. The best account of the uses that Smith's story has been put to.

JAMESON, J. FRANKLIN. *The History of Historical Writing in America.* Boston: Houghton Mifflin Co., 1891. Still useful for its evaluation of Smith's writings.

JONES, HOWARD MUMFORD. *The Literature of Virginia in the Seventeenth Century. Memoirs of the American Academy of Arts and Sciences*, XIX (1941–46). Part 2. Boston, 1946. Second edition, Charlottesville: University Press of Virginia, 1968. Twenty-two pages are devoted to Smith. Somewhat impressionistic, but useful because of the context.

KRAUS, MICHAEL. *A History of American History.* New York: Farrar & Rinehart, 1937. Revised as *The Writing of American History.* Norman: University of Oklahoma Press. 1953. A brief evaluation of Smith as historian.

LANKFORD, JOHN, ED. *Captain John Smith's America: Selections From His Writings.* New York: Harper & Row, 1967. Includes a twenty-one page essay on Smith. One of the best recent accounts of Smith as historian.

MCCABE, W. GORDON. "Captain John Smith's Travels," *Oxford and Cambridge Review*, #2 (1907), 3–17. Attractive general essay.

MORISON, SAMUEL ELIOT. *Builders of the Bay Colony.* Boston: Houghton Mifflin Co., 1958. Chapter I: "Promoters and Precursors: Richard Hakluyt, Captain John Smith, and Morton of Merrymount." Not wholly fair in its remarks on Smith's veracity but useful nonetheless.

MORSE, JARVIS M. *American Beginnings.* Washington: Public Affairs Press, 1952. Comments knowledgeably on Smith as historian.

———. "Captain John Smith and His Critics: A Chapter in Colonial Historiography," *Journal of Southern History*, I (1935), 123–37. Very valuable survey of Smith's writings and commentators on them.

MORTON, RICHARD L. *Colonial Virginia.* 2 volumes. Chapel Hill: University of North Carolina Press, 1960. Full history of the colony. Morton praises Smith's work as leader of Jamestown.

POINDEXTER, CHARLES. *Captain John Smith and His Critics.* Richmond: Privately printed, 1893. Partial to Smith, but intelligent and worth reading.

ROWSE, A. L. *The Elizabethans and America.* New York: Harper and Brothers, 1959. Important background study, with passing references to Smith.

ROZWENC, EDWIN C. "Captain John Smith's Image of America," *William and Mary Quarterly,* 3rd series, XVI (1959), 26–36. Perceptive study. Argues that Smith gave the English a "vision of America as a place in which to achieve personal honor and glory."

SIMMS, WILLIAM GILMORE. *The Life of Captain John Smith.* Boston: John Philbrick, 1854. Important only as a sample of nineteenth-century attitudes. Sentimental, uncritical.

SMITH, BRADFORD. *Captain John Smith: His Life & Legend.* Philadelphia: J. B. Lippincott Company, 1953. Though superseded by Barbour's book, still worth consulting. Includes as an appendix "Captain John Smith's Hungary and Transylvania," by Laura Polanyi Striker.

STRIKER, LAURA P. and BRADFORD SMITH. "The Rehabilitation of Captain John Smith," *Journal of Southern History,* XXVIII (1962), 474–81. Best treatment of the subject, but written before most of Barbour's studies.

TAYLOR, E. G. R. *Late Tudor and Early Stuart Geography, 1583–1650.* London: Methuen & Co., 1934. Considers Smith in the context of geographical literature.

TYLER, MOSES COIT. *A History of American Literature, 1607–1765.* New York: G. P. Putnam's Sons, 1878; New York: Collier Books, 1962. Still the standard history; whole chapter is devoted to Smith.

WHARTON, HENRY. *The Life of John Smith, English Soldier.* Translated from the Latin Manuscript with an Essay on Captain John Smith in Seventeenth Century Literature by Laura Polanyi Striker. Chapel Hill: University of North Carolina Press, 1957. Interesting but of no great value, for Wharton was often badly confused. Useful if thin introduction.

B. *Background Information*

ANDREWS, CHARLES M. *The Colonial Period of American History.* 4 volumes. New Haven: Yale University Press, 1934. First volume provides a very helpful overview of America's colonization.

BROWN, ALEXANDER, ED. *The Genesis of the United States.* 2 volumes. Boston: Houghton, Mifflin and Company, 1891. Valuable collection of documents relating to Jamestown colony. Brown was unsympathetic with Smith.

CRAVEN, FRANK WESLEY. *The Southern Colonies in the Seventeenth-Century, 1607–1689.* Baton Rouge: Louisiana State University Press, 1949. The best modern study, incorporating recent research.

CULLIFORD, S. G. *William Strachey, 1572–1621.* Charlottesville: The University Press of Virginia, 1965. Biography of a colonist and writer whose career was in some ways parallel to Smith's.

INNES, A. D. *The Maritime and Colonial Expansion of England Under the Stuarts (1603–1714).* London: Samson Low, Marston, and Co., 1932. Considers Virginia colony in a broad context.

JONES, HOWARD MUMFORD. "The Colonial Impulse: An Analysis of the 'Promotion' Literature of Colonization," *Proceedings of the American Philosophical Society,* XC (1946), 131–61. Since much of what Smith wrote was promotion literature, a relevant and useful study.

———. *O Strange New World. American Culture: The Formative Years.* New York: The Viking Press, 1964. Very important background study, discursive and suggestive.

NOTESTEIN, WALLACE. *The English People on the Eve of Colonization, 1602–1630.* New York: Harper and Brothers, 1954. Chapters on Smith's England, leading to one on "The Companies and Colonization."

PARKER, JOHN. *Books to Build an Empire. A Bibliographical History of English Overseas Interests to 1620.* Amsterdam: N. Israel, 1965. A solid and scholarly treatment of the topic to which the title clearly points.

PENNINGTON, LOREN E. *Hakluytus Posthumus: Samuel Purchas and the Promotion of Overseas Expansion.* Emporia State Research Studies, XIV (1966). One of the few modern studies of Purchas, Smith's associate.

PENROSE, BOIES. *Travel and Discovery in the Renaissance, 1420–1620.* Cambridge: Harvard University Press, 1952. Lively general study.

QUINN, DAVID B. *Raleigh and the British Empire.* London: The English Universities Press, 1962. Smith's and Raleigh's interests overlapped.

———, ED. *The Roanoke Voyages, 1584–1590.* Two volumes. London: The Hakluyt Society, 1955. Collection of documents, skillfully edited, including Hariot's book.

ROWSE, A. L. *The Expansion of Elizabethan England.* New York: St. Martin's Press, 1955. Includes valuable and fresh chapter on American colonization.

STORY, IRVING C. "Elizabethan Prelude," *Pacific University Studies in Literature,* #3, November, 1942. Relates Smith to Hakluyt.

WILLIAMSON, JAMES A. *The Tudor Age.* 3rd edition. New York: David McKay Company, 1964. Emphasizes exploration and colonization.

WRIGHT, LOUIS B. *Middle-Class Culture in Elizabethan England.* Ithaca: Cornell University Press, 1958. On the vogue of travel literature.

———. *Religion and Empire: The Alliance between Piety and Commerce in English Expansion, 1558–1625.* Chapel Hill: University of North Carolina Press, 1943.

———. *The Colonial Search for a Southern Eden.* University: University of Alabama Press, 1953. A brief but thoughtful study.

———, ED. *The Elizabethans' America: A Collection of Early Reports by Englishmen on the New World.* Cambridge: Harvard University Press, 1965. Includes four selections from Smith among its forty-two pieces.

Index

Adams, Henry, 94, 131
Arber, Edward, 100
Archer, Gabriel, 45, 53

Bacon, Francis, 42, 109
Barbour, Philip L., 1, 2, 4, 48, 90, 94, 97, 103, 127, 128, 130, 131, 132
Benét, Stephen Vincent, 2, 4, 125, 126, 133
Bermuda, 26, 32, 40, 72–74, 75
Bradford, William, 63, 75, 87, 123
Brereton, John, 22–24, 37, 45, 66, 67, 127
Brown, Alexander, 52, 72, 128, 129, 130
Butler, Nathaniel, 73–74, 130

Cabot, John and Sebastian, 13, 15, 16, 66
Cape Cod, 22–24, 27
Charles, Prince, 74, 102, 103–4, 109, 111
Coleridge, Samuel Taylor, 30, 127–28
Cotton, Robert, 96
Coke, Edward, 110
Crashaw, William, 27, 127
Crèvecoeur, St. Jean de, 121, 133
Cusson, George, 61

Davies, John, 104
Deane, Charles, 94, 131
De Bry, Theodore, 17, 54
Dee, John, 75, 111
de la Warre, Thomas West, Lord, 40, 70
DeSoto, Fernando, 30
Donne, John, 33, 64
Drake, Francis, 13
Drayton, Michael, 15–16

Eames, Wilberforce, 110, 133
Egerton, John, 110
Elizabeth I, 15, 19, 31, 41

Ferneza, Francisco, 97, 99
Florida, 13, 16, 29
Florio, John, 15

Fotherby, Martin, 64
Franklin, Benjamin, 121
Frobisher, Martin, 17, 66

Gates, Thomas, 26, 40, 41, 53, 73
Gilbert, Humphrey, 14, 22, 66
Glenn, Keith, 58, 129, 130
Gorges, Ferdinando, 26, 41–42
Gosnold, Bartholomew, 22, 23, 24, 37, 39, 66
Guiana, 19–22, 36, 65, 76

Haie, Edward, 14, 126
Hakluyt, Richard, 15–16, 19, 22, 24, 29–30, 65, 66, 67, 87, 126, 127, 130
Hamor, Ralph, 70
Hariot, Thomas, 17–19, 37, 45, 55, 57, 66
Hertford, Earl of, see Seymour, John
Howe, Henry F., 103, 132

Indians, American, 18, 21, 23–24, 25, 47–51, 56–57, 58–61, 66, 71, 79–83

Jameson, J. Franklin, 72, 130
Jamestown, 28, 37, 49, 50, 51, 52, 53, 65, 70, 80
Johnson, Edward, 63
Jones, Howard Mumford, 1, 52, 53, 55, 58, 94, 123, 129, 131, 133
Jourdain, Sylvester, 73

Kendall, George, 38, 39
Kropf, Lewis, 94, 131

Lane, Ralph, 19, 66
Lankford, John, 123, 133
Lewis, C. S., 21, 127
Lewis, Paul, 1

Maine, 23, 25, 26, 27, 41, 103
Mainwaring, Henry, 90, 131
Markham, Gervase, 88, 90
Martha's Vineyard, 23

Martin, John, 38, 39
McCary, Ben, 55, 60, 129
Mercator, Gerdhardus, 15
Miller, Perry, 60, 129
Montaigne, Michel de, 15
Morse, Jarvis M., 78, 94, 129, 130, 131
Morison, Samuel Eliot, 103, 132
"Mourt," 75, 130

Nantucket, 24
Nevis, 76
New England, exploration of, 22–26,
41–42
Newfoundland, 13, 14, 42
Newport, Christopher, 37, 38, 40, 49,
50, 52, 73, 78, 81, 83–84, 85, 86
North Carolina, 17–19, 27, 65, 66
Norton, Robert, 34, 92
Norwood, Richard, 73

Pearce, Roy Harvey, 59, 129
Percy, George, 45, 86
Pilgrims, 42, 103, 111, 116
Pocahontas, 32, 39, 47, 51, 57, 72, **84–
85**, 103, 112, 122–23
Pocahontas story, 80–81
Poe, Edgar Allan, 19
Powhatan, 39, 40, 47, 48, 49, 50, 51, 52,
61, 81, 84, 85, 86
Purchas, Samuel, 26, 30, 31, 32, 42–43,
55, 56, 64, 65, 67, 87, 90–91, 96–97,
127, 128, 130, 131

Quinn, David B., 17, 126, 127

Raleigh, Walter, 14, 15, 17, 18, 19–22,
26, 66, 127
Ratcliffe, John, 38, 39, 53, 94
Richmond and Lenox, Duchess of, 42,
64
Roanoke colony, *see* North Carolina
Rolfe, John, 42, 69, 81
Rosier, James, 24, 25, 26, 45, 67
Rowse, A. L., 16, 114, 126, 127, 133

Saltonstall, Samuel, 88
Sandys, Edwin, 73
Sandys, George, 64
Seymour, Edward, Earl of Hertford, 41,
42
Shakespeare, William, 26
Sidney, Philip, 14

Smith, Bradford, 1, 2, 48, 64, 81, 94, 128,
129, 130, 131
Smith, John, early years, 35, 95; Conti-
nental travels, 36, 95–96; Virginia
years, 36–41, 46–52; years in England,
41–44, 53–57, 63–64, 109–10; New
England voyage, 41, 106; death, 53,
113; question of his reliability, 94,
101; marring of his writings by subjective preoccupation, 76–77, 110–11; as
propagandist, 57, 104–6, 107–8, 110,
116, 117–18; on future of America,
116, 121

WRITINGS OF:

Accidence, An, 34, 43, 88–91, 119
*Advertisements for the unexperienced
Planters,* 33, 34, 43, 78, 102, 113–
18, 119, 120, 124
Description of New England, A, 32,
33, 41, 74, 78, 103–9, 110, 117, 119,
121, 123–24
Generall Historie, The, 22, 29, 31, 32,
33, 34, 42, 43, 46, 47, 61, 62, 63–87,
96, 112, 113, 117, 119, 122, 123
Map of Virginia, A, 22, 29, 31, 32, 33,
39, 41, 45, 50, 54–62, 67–68, 119,
121–22
New Englands Trials, 32, 36, 75, 109–
12, 117
Sea Grammar, A, 43, 90–91, 119
True Relation, A, 32, 39, 45–53, 62,
78, 123
True Travels, The, 33, 43, 65, 75–76,
88, 94–102, 113–14, 117, 119
Verses, 91–93, 115, 131
Projected book on the sea, 113
Smythe, John, 63
Somers, George, 26, 28, 40, 41, 73
Strachey, William, 23, 26–29, 40, 6̱
Striker, Laura, 94
Symonds, William, 45, 54, 55, 86

Taylor, E. G. R., 16, 30, 106–7, 126, 127,
132
Taylor, John, 91–92
Tyler, Moses Coit, 1, 27, 52, 83, 94, 122,
127, 130, 133

Virginia, exploration of, 38, 39, 46–48,
50

Virginia Company, 36–38, 39, 40, 48, 53, 54, 59, 63, 69, 70, 79, 83

Waterhouse, Edward, 70
Waymouth, George, 24
Whitbourne, Richard, 75
White, John, 17, 55
Williamson, James A., 17, 126

Willoughby, Robert, Lord, 35, 36, 82
Wingfield, Edward Maria, 37, 38, 39, 45, 52, 79, 85, 131
Winslow, Edward, 75
Winthrop, John, 63, 116, 133
Wither, George, 104
Wright, Louis B., 16, 31, 126, 127, 128, 129, 133

About the Author

Everett H. Emerson, Professor of English and Director of Honors at the University of Massachusetts, is a leading student of early American literature. He was the first chairman of the Modern Language Association's group on American literature of the seventeenth and eighteenth centuries (1969) and is editor of its publication, *Early American Literature*. Emerson's writings include the Twayne's United States Authors (volume on John Cotton) and the recent *English Puritanism from John Hooper to John Milton* (Duke University Press). In addition to publishing numerous scholarly articles and reviews, he has edited selections from John Milton's prose and prepared facsimile editions of works by Thomas Hooker and John Cotton.

Professor Emerson studied at Dartmouth, Harvard, Duke, and Louisiana State, and has taught at Lehigh, New York University, and Florida Presbyterian College, where he was a member of the founding faculty.